Like a Thrill

Writings from around the world
that will glow your mind

Janet Kaufmann

Conscious Dreams
P U B L I S H I N G

Like a Thrill

Wie ein Rausch / Alla corrente del vento

Copyright © 2024: Janet Kaufmann

First Printed in United Kingdom 2024

Published by Conscious Dreams Publishing
www.consciousdreamspublishing.com

Edited by Elise Abram

Translated into German and Italian language by Janet Kaufmann

Typeset by Oksana Kosovan

ISBN: 978-1-915522-81-8

The only revolution that can happen is from within our hearts

Contents

I. North Wind

I Am an Artist

I am an artist
I need lots of rest
For my spirit to recover in his vessel
On this physical plane
Where we came
To love again

Isle of Skye, Scotland, October 2022

Tick Tack Tock

Tick tack tock
Abolish all the clocks
Time in a frame
Doesn't suit my name
Earth and sky be my guide
Sun and moonlight
Shine my way
Must live day by day

Isle of Skye, Scotland, September 2022

Talk, Talk, Talk

Talk, talk, talk
Oh, all the people's talk
Senseless chatter
Weather, neighbour, prime minister
One more beer, chatter without fear
Next day's morning
Silence unspoken
Where is your action?
Silly distractions
Never mind the weather
Let's build something better

Isle of Skye, Scotland, October 2022

Wandersouls

We, the wandersouls, do not travel for fun alone; it's way more than that. What might look like a holiday to you is actually work, as well. While others sit in offices or stock up grocery shelves, we restore and cleanse distorted energies of entire lands and tribes, connect places, timelines and dimensions, and anchor cosmic consciousness while we expand into our own unlimitedness, love and Oneness with all that is, and at night, I happen to go to work at the local pub. Not that different from you, and I did the supermarket shelves and office jobs, too, but no more human slavery for money, hey! We might not speak about our cosmic job much, and most is done subconsciously, and you might do it, too, or do you know where you venture out in your dreams at night?

Isle of Skye, Scotland, September 2022

Wet, Cold, Blue Ocean

Before my eyes, a wet, cold, blue ocean. Today, short waves, a splashing and slapping on the large, round pebble stones in front of the quay. Swash, swash. The beach is almost submerged. The sea is rippled today, rocking a few dozen boats. Small and big ones, blue, yellow, red, green, brown fishing boats. Some sway so much you almost feel dizzy. One comes in, one goes out. I wonder what kind of fish they caught. I want to come along. Maybe I'll meet a fisherman. I walk along the quay against a stiff breeze. Not a soul, far and wide, on this cold November Monday evening. Dim lights are coming out of the colourful houses, lining up along the pier. Everyone is at home. I am the only spectator in the cinema tonight.

Isle of Skye, Scotland, November 2022

The Fisherman

The magic of that little place—it still exists, and you will find it when you don't rush to one of the tourist attractions. So, I am sitting here on this little rocky beach on which the tourists often miss stepping while occupied taking pictures from the pier, and others, sitting and drinking in the pub, so I get it all to myself, with the seabirds diving in and out, and the gentle crashing of the waves that rock the handful of fishing boats framed by the colourful facades, the pink, the blue, the green, the yellow cottages, each of them having their own story to tell, and so, I meet the friendly fisherman going out on his boat on this beautiful, warm October day.

Isle of Skye, Scotland, October 2022

Rainbow Bridge

Life is all about improvisation, adaptation to the ever-present moment unfolding in a million different possibilities. It is good to be 'stuck'. It's great not to have my car. To walk that empty road. On a cold but stunning November day. See the first snow on the mountain tops. Feel the earth under my feet. The energy running through my body. The fresh breeze on my cheeks. Saying 'Hi' to the sheep by the side of the road. Feeling my breath slow down because I am in nature, in awe of Creation, walking through the rainbow bridge. The prison of society and culture becomes an irrelevant drop somewhere over the horizon. It's nice to get a lift from these lovely Croatian, Ukrainian and Scottish locals and travellers sharing the excitement of life. It's great to get out of that car again, to turn around, see the clouds coming in, and walk ahead of them into the light. Through the rain in the dark. Back into the light. Always back to the light.

Isle of Skye, Scotland, November 2022

Spiritual Awakening

I must have been about sixteen when I first discovered and loved the other world, the nonphysical world. We are actually there all the time as babies and children. I remember how I escaped from home to lie on my back on a snowy hill, looking into the sky in a desert of white, puffin' a cigarette that made me feel dizzy—a state that I somehow liked because it detached me from the physical world, the world I knew. People drink and do drugs to get relief from their painful physical existence for a little while that is painful when we cut ourselves off from spirit, from Source, from nature, from our true selves, from what and who we really are. Back in the day, I overdid the drinks and dope, too, because I couldn't get enough of being in that place where I felt a greater sense, a depth that was missing in our physical, everyday programmed lives—a place where I felt more at home until, gladly, my higher-self decided to have a spiritual awakening in my thirties instead of dying from a life of Rock 'n' Roll that catapulted me right where I belonged, on my soul's journey in a very heavy, extreme way; that was the shift I needed. In a technical way, it opened up my chakras, the third eye, for me to See, and all of the other chakras, with the greatest life force running through me: Kundalini energy, cosmic energy. An opening and activation of your energy centres—that is all that a spiritual awakening really is, and it's about time to get that right. It's an opening of your chakras realigning you to Source, to nature, to the cosmos, to who you really are, and nothing will ever be the same again, and you will never need to do drugs or drink (I don't) again because now, you can be in that holy space naturally, and stay there with a little bit of regular healthy spiritual practice like meditation, introspection, expressing your soul, grounding in nature, avoiding anything toxic. It's as simple as that. Now, I've lost the plot of what I actually wanted to say, which is why I love things that taste and feel a little cosmic besides the earthly things that I love just as much. They are, in fact, interconnected, and I like to point out the importance of the combination of both in everyday life and society that is missing, which is the reason why the world is out of balance. This is why I praise freedom and deep love, why I love unlimited travel, and epic adventure, just life. Just living life outside of this stupid little cardboard box they try to put you in, and I was never meant not to break it.

Isle of Skye, Scotland, October 2022

New School

Being a teacher by profession, I do not believe in our school system anymore, and I am having doubts if I want to engage in this form ever again. I believe that learning must happen naturally, without too fixed timetables, walls and frames and through discovery and exploration instead of indoctrination to raise children who are able to think for themselves, form an opinion and build a future and ways of life to realize themselves and be happy. The new learning could occur in the form of a community, where the adults and elders share their wisdom, various skills, gifts and talents with the children which can be anything, really, from gardening, dancing, singing, building, drawing, meditating, horse riding, cooking and so on practised by the adults in their everyday lives instead of working for a job to pay their bills only. This way, the learning becomes more natural as well as fun together, with all different age groups and community builds values like love, respect, empathy, integrity, and communion instead of insecure young people and unhappy adults competing with one another. There must be access and direct interaction to different fields of interest for the kids, like arts, literature, philosophy, foreign languages and cultures, history, botanics and so on for the children to choose and study by themselves or together instead of following stiff curriculums made up by people too long ago, who often have no clue about real life, and instead of being put under a constant pressure to perform. They must have lots of space to do nothing at all or whatever they wish to do because this is how great ideas are born and because we are born to be free. The school system is out of date if you are a visionary, too, if you dare to be free.

Isle of Skye, Scotland, November 2022

See Their Hearts
When You Open Yours

Do not mind the miserable people who don't like you because you are happy, and don't let that ever stop you from making other people happy. Like the whiskey drinker who said he loved me and how nice it was to see him smile when I was standing at the bar at noon, just like that, because I must never ever separate myself from all kinds of people but stand amidst life, and because my colleague in the kitchen can be just as enlightened as the one who openly declares to be so, and I must not judge who and what I am not but see the equality of our hearts instead of the superficial differences, and I must bring everybody together; that is what I love. Like the guy who tried in vain to hitchhike in the same spot as I did today, and, of course, I invited him to come along in the lift I hitched for myself, and how it made his day as the driver was going all the way where he was trying to get all day. That made me happy to see him happy, and the driver was happy, too, because he hadn't spoken to anyone today, and so was my Irish friend I went for a walk with today, and the Scottish one I'll meet tomorrow. Making each other happy, whatever their beliefs, origin or status, and seeing how we are all one family is the most beautiful thing I have learned, especially on my travels and by immersing myself in all different kinds of environments and cultures, and there is always the chance to make someone happy, even if it is just some stranger who is out there on the road just like you, and never ever judge anyone by their looks, but see their hearts when you open yours.

Isle of Skye, Scotland, October 2022

Put your Love
Into Something Greater

We can love so many things: my neighbour, my neighbour's cat, my mother, your daughter, my friend, the stranger on the street who responds to my smile. We can love women, men, children and elders, animals and plants, rocks, the stars, the sun, the rain, the wind. What we love is a part of ourselves. I feel the love for the wind and the cosmos with every cell of my body. It makes me greater than I am. Love expands. Must I have sex with that which I love? Yes and no. Sex could change that connection. That friendship. Love is ethereal, and sex is physical, and yes, we can combine the two, but only if there is love. When it becomes addictive, then love is no longer free, or shall we just let love flow? There are sooo many different stages and depths of love, and I believe that if it is true, deep love, you must let it flow and merge and rise together. If it is friendship-love, I believe it is not worth sharing on a physical level, that ever-confusing, mixed-up topic leading to open relationship commitments, betrayal and lies—or do you know of a hippie commune as in the 70s that became happily ever after? While being high, yes, it's cool, but things look different the next day. Why have a relationship in the first place if you want other partners at the same time? Why can we not just be friends, then? Is that not co-dependency, being unable to be with or without one another? I believe there are endless forms of living love, also in female-male friendships, that we can extend. Create something together. Put your love into something Greater.

Isle of Skye, Scotland, November 2022

Halloween Party

Sorry, I'm not coming to your Halloween party
I think you look strange
I don't find it funny
I lie awake at night and download poems
And you think I am strange
It's not funny
We only carry names
The stars know you better

Isle of Skye, Scotland, November 2022

In Between Places

Just a few of the countless things I learned from nomading through many different countries, years, and experiences are that moving from place to place lies in my human nature, and if I ever settle, it will only be for a few months until I move on to my next place or adventure instead of making my home my castle controlled by the material world of collecting and consuming more and more things that I do not need in life or getting too fat and lazy within my routines and comfort zones. If I'd settle, it will never be in a little concrete box ever again because as soon as I open my eyes, I wish to step with my feet on Mother Earth, see the horizon and walk towards the sun. I also learned that if the people don't integrate you or doors don't open for you where you live, or if you haven't made any real friends, it is time to move on. However, no place in the world will ever be a substitute for your home, your choice of incarnation, your soil, where you were born and raised. This doesn't mean we must be bound to that place forever because true love knows no attachment, not to people, not to places, not to things. We can enjoy and live in or between different places opposite what society tells us, to be a prisoner of our jobs, houses, belongings, circles, schedules, of time and place in a frame. Long gone concept that only suits someone who has truly never tasted freedom.

Isle of Skye, Scotland, November 2022

My Moody, Bonnie Scotland

My moody, bonnie Scotland
Our remaining time is running short
Sweet melancholia of the lonely north
You made me look into the deepest corners
of my soul
Your rough, rugged beauty
Has comforted me in the darkest of the days
For the brave ones
To find the light

Isle of Skye, Scotland, December 2022

Bumpy, Noisy Bus

I lay my tired body on the four back
seats to sleep
Watching snowed-in mountain ranges merging
with a white sky passing by
Carry me, carry me far away
Bumpy noisy, bus rocking me into sleep
I'll wake up in another place
With a new life
Keep on riding the waves

Isle of Skye, Scotland, December 2022

II. West Wards

Rio, Downtown!

Listening to the beautiful piano music from the lower floor that is playing a concert in tune with the warm rain dropping on my terrace while I am lying in my bed in the Hotel Americano, which is not at all American but very Brazilian, and the thousand, colourful images of the day are shooting through my head like a buzz, just as the day was a blissful buzz. My first day in Brazil, in Rio de Janeiro, and despite the voices of others and the American tourist at the reception who said that Rio is dangerous and they rob you straight away, I threw myself into the streets, into the flood, the firework, into the bustle of life. Not in the world-famous Copacabana or Ipanema district, where I cancelled my hotel at the last minute, but in the real downtown, where the Rio de Janeiro people live. *Oh, Jesus, que bênção foi ser pobre!* I walked on the street and felt no danger, unlike the warnings of the American who thought he was better than the Brazilians, and just because he robs people—he works in finances—doesn't mean that I must get robbed, too! Everybody creates their own experience! I saw them, the Rio de Janeiro people, and they smiled at me, and I felt welcome. Beautiful people, friendly people—I saw their hearts, and they touched mine. There is so much beauty in the mix of the Indigenous, African and European heritage. There is so much heavy history and rich culture on this continent, and yet they seem light at heart, and from every corner, there is music—samba, reggaeton, and other loud, great music—and I saw some amazing street art. I am in the old town, in the heart of the city, with all the street parties. Many people sleep in the streets here, too, and there is a lot of poverty and drug problems. I've heard the shots from the favelas, but that's life; it's better than living in a bubble and sitting in a snobby Copacabana hotel with tourists at a boring hotel bar! I'd rather be here in the middle of life with the people—I love them all. I'll also check out

Ipanema and Copacabana, and I'll love it, too, just like the Brazilians love their beaches and tomorrow I'll go up Sugarloaf Mountain, but now I have to sleep with my little crystal toucan bird smiling friendlily at me; who intrigued me when I saw him at the street market—the rainforest is calling me, too! The adventure on my doorstep. I am in South America, and I couldn't be any happier!

Rio de Janeiro, Brazil, January 2023

Rio High

Four days in Rio feel like an entire lifetime anywhere else! A constant high! I am so much in love with this, the most beautiful city in the world, and its people, lifestyle, *joie de vivre*, madness, contrasts and Oh, my god!—its music! Samba bossa nova, reggae! Life here just happens on the street, and everything is an improvisation or an adventure, and although I should be tired, I feel energized, even though I don't really like city life, here it feels different as if they all stuck together as one big family in this crazy life. People just make a fire in the middle of the street to cook something in a can and have dinner on the pavement—why not?! They sell the best caipirinhas on each street corner, and they cost only 50 cents! Since I don't drink, I have coconut water all the time out of a coconut straight from the tree, and I have been eating tons of exotic fruit since I got here—lost some weight, already. You just dance a lot here, and life generally feels so light—actually, every day feels like a party! I just wanted to go to bed, but the drums are so loud on the streets that I just cannot resist.

Rio de Janeiro, Brazil, January 2023

Brazil

Hmm Brazil
I will remember you
By the smell of your rich coffee that tastes of
lush green mountains in a thousand shades
of green merging with the emerald sea
By your beautiful mix of happy people of
all colours
By your samba, bossa nova and sertanejo
By your exotic fruit and flowers
By your mesmerizing drumming
From people who came in wooden boats
from far away long time ago
By your overabundant exuberance
By your craziness
By your *beleza*
By your big, precious heart

Costa Verde, Brazil, January 2023

Wind, Carry Me

Been hanging out with some locals in this hippie-vibe beach town that made me a part of their daily *asados* — South American barbecue — and music sessions in the house of El Barba, an 84-year-old poet and revolutionary artist, where free spirits gather together and share their ideas about the world, and lots of Tango, Fado, Murga, Candombe, Choclo, Son, Salsa, Bossa Nova... . What a treat! Now, letting the wind carry me onwards. Be wild and free like a Uruguayan horse.

Rocha, Uruguay, January 2023

Uruguay

And I learned to flow
Gracias Uruguay
País del Río de los pajaros pintados
River river
Water water
Mar y Sol
Now Flow

Rocha, Uruguay, January 2023

El Camino

I have surrendered to this most epic journey, the biggest trip of my lifetime so far, through South America on my own. From the first part in Brazil that felt great but a little challenging with the tropical heat, lots of mosquitos, the noise, one sick and many short nights and with my phone falling off the boat to the ground of the emerald sea and found after 24 hours by a local diver who is said to find everything, without equipment, of course, and surprisingly, with my British and German SIM cards saved, but the message was clear. The voyage has evolved into an epic ride, intense and fast, with lots of unforeseeable moves and adventures, learning to surf the high tides that give you that thrill, that reminds you of how life should feel most of the time, like an ecstasy and not like a slumber or a struggle. The moment I gave up my plans and stopped using the internet on my phone to find places to stay or where to go, the moment when I surrendered to the flow, doors opened up everywhere I went with special encounters and connections along the way, guiding me from one station to the next, one step leading to the next—genius but often ignored principle of life, of embracing nothing but the very present moment without expectations or too many plans. This is how the path—*el camino*—opened up: as I am walking it. Genius universal principle, not only of this voyage but of life, letting it unfold by itself in its magic by little expectations, embracing each moment. This is how I have ended up in the cottage of my dreams where I am staying at the moment, which costs a penny in the *Sierra de Cordoba* in the heart of Argentina—real beautiful, raw Argentina. Not a tourist far and wide who meanwhile all flock to expensive and touristy Patagonia. They still have these old-fashioned, tiny grocery stores here, where they pack food into small quantities, and everything is organic and super tasty. Whatever shop I walked into, people started conversations with me. They are incredibly friendly and heartful here, the complete opposite of how I experienced the *porteños*, the people of Buenos Aires. It is wonderful to see the spirit of community and life in its simplicity and beauty when capitalism hasn't penetrated society as much and spoiled the good things in life—when love and togetherness drive the people instead of greed and egoism. The people look really happy here, and going out and music are important parts of everyday life everywhere in South America at all times. Shops close at midnight, and the Argentineans go to bed really late, and, like in Uruguay, they drive around in these old, cool cars, and they love to share their *Mate*—the local's drink made of herbs—which is a big part of the Argentinian identity. The cottage where I am currently staying in the middle of pure nature is sitting on the oldest rock in the world—well, it stretches right into the house. I can touch it from my bed since my new friend, Marcos, a cool guy who travelled the world himself before building this little haven that he shares with visitors, integrated the spirit of the landscape. It is sitting on a subterranean stream that gives you vivid, colourful dreams, he says. The big, wild river is at a short walking distance, where the locals bathe, and that shaped the landscape with beautiful pools to swim in, including sandy beaches. All I hear here are birds and the concert of the crickets while gazing at the most amazing sky of stars at night. Coming back to where we come from — nature — where everything feels rich and divine beyond the illusion of time.

Mina Clavero, Argentina, January 2023

Free Roaming

I would like to roam around the world forever. I love the move, the change of scenery, the traits and the cultures of the people, the change of food, the flora, the fauna and the climates. The smiles and open hearts stay the same wherever I go. I love to follow rivers through valleys and mountain ranges stretching to the seas, crossing oceans, hopping from islands beyond to the unknown. Sometimes, I get 'stuck' in a place for a reason. Reflecting upon myself, the journey and gazing at the stars for a bit longer. Will I spot a spaceship?

Somewhere in Argentina, January 2023

One World

Whoever it was that told me to fear the foreign, the far, the other, the unknown, was a liar. Your world is my world, and my world is your world. Nothing more beautiful than sharing my lunch in this public kitchen in town today with the locals, the kids, the elders, the travellers—one of these special moments of travel. I had the best Titicaca Lake trout ever. They eat very well here, gild their teeth, dress up a lot, and are really sweet, but they call Bolivia a third-world country because they blow the money up their own a*ses only. See who is happier. The more I travel, the more I feel a part of it all. Distance and differences are just an illusion of the physical world someone fearful came up with. Not in my world. Our world. People here don't treat me any differently because I see no difference in them. I see beauty. I see love. I have been travelling with little money, not caring at all how much will be left; to worry is for the fearful ones, too. Travel makes you rich inside. For good.

Copacabana, Titicaca Lake, Bolivia, February 2023

Bridging Worlds

Machu Picchu was closed for two months, and even Peruvian tour guides told me just two weeks ago that it is closed until further notice, and travel in Peru isn't possible because of political unrest; they said it wouldn't reopen before April. I haven't seen one single demonstration, and they reopened Machu Picchu surprisingly two days ago when I purchased a ticket that is usually sold-out months ahead, and I had Machu Picchu pretty much to myself. If I would have listened to others, I would never have come to Peru. However, I did listen to my intuition instead that told me to just go, and my passage via Lake Titicaca and through the mountains was smooth and special. It felt as if it had been facilitated. In fact, the whole trip in South America did/does. Why? Because I have followed my heart, which is when doors open. Why do so many people want to visit Machu Picchu? One of the Seven World Wonders to tick off your bucket list? I hate that word. It makes a really good picture of you posing next to it, too. Why did I come to Machu Picchu? Well, I heard the call. Bridging worlds and dimensions. I am not a tourist; I am a traveller; I am an explorer; and I am a cosmic child. We all are, whether you remember or not.

Machu Picchu, Peru, February 2023

Cosmic Wonder

Damn! Why would I be sick with diarrhoea just one day previous to my climb of Machu Picchu from eating this mesmerising, exotic yellow rainforest fruit unknown to me that produces a 'cleanse of the body', they told me later? Diarrhoea, to be fair! So, I climb my Machu Picchu, nevertheless. Of course, after the 10,000 miles I made to get here, quite exhausted and tired due to the magical yellow fruit, I get all emotional approaching the site due to my physical state, or is it Machu Picchu that overwhelms me? Amazed, I wonder through the site, passing by small tourist groups being bombarded by tons of information from their tourist guide, thinking to myself that I could never record all of that information, so I hang around the central temple of the Sun God for quite some time. I feel something strong and intriguing here. I leave after a while, but I come back and continue to stick around the special place until one of the guardians takes note of me and asks me if I wish to meditate in the shaman's ritual temple facing the sun temple, inaccessible to tourists normally. Tired and stroked by the Incan sun, it is exactly the place where I need to be, so he brings me into the sacred temple in secret, where I sit down in the shade of the huge stones, with my body feeling relieved and I just breathe, breathe, breathe, and it happens: my consciousness opens up to the higher, to the lower and to all other dimensions and to all times, the past and the future, are all here now. I receive the cosmic energies and secrets through my crown chakra into my body, to my root into the earth and vice versa, from my root up to the heavens, and I bridge the worlds into the now. I am a cosmic wonder, and I create miracles yesterday, today, tomorrow and forever. This is the beginning of the New Age. It is here, and it is now. I am Every Now.

Machu Picchu, Peru, February 2023

Citizen of the World

You change your home every few days or weeks. So does the food, as it changes with the places you roam. You eat fruits and other strange things you never saw before. You don't mind sometimes having your instant coffee cold, eating with your hands on the bed because you don't have a table, and you like it because you feel free while you look outside the window of your sweet little guesthouse that costs you much less than renting a house at home, and you look out at the hills and the slogan, *Viva el Peru*, written there, with the peaceful dawn slowly setting over the red roofs of Cuzco, and you feel like a citizen of the world. You are not sure if you should stop now—sometimes you wish this trip would never end—you could go on and on forever, every time braver, wiser, calmer, happier, and you know that sometimes your body gets tired, and you let it be tired. You don't rush around only when you need to, and you know when you have to pull yourself together and must sometimes run, then you will, and if you still miss the only bus, you go, 'F*ck it,' and you enjoy being stuck, and you are not sure which is better—the excitement of moving, gazing at the changing landscapes, heights, climates, vegetation, and traits and customs of the people, or dwelling in the one place you become familiar with and discover its secrets at a deeper look—but you know it is beyond epic, life. And your major concern when you are thinking about what to wear today is to choose between the colour of red or green because all you need fits into a tiny backpack, and if something is missing, you just go and buy it on the streets, and if your favourite hat gets blown away by the wind on the ship you are on, you release it, and you gift it to the silver sea of the *Rio de la Plata*, and you trust that you will find an even better one. And you leave the new one that you bought in Bolivia to whoever will find it in Peru because it doesn't suit your style in Colombia, and you will find an even cooler one in Panama. And sometimes, you make new friends along the way, and you tell them goodbye, and you do not know if you'll ever meet again, but you'll love them forever.

Cuzco, Peru, February 2023

Cuzco

This trip feels so epic because it is not limited in time or in any other beliefs. The world is my living room. Sometimes, I feel like flying, like the South American condor circling high, to the Peruvian flute that is playing in the background scene, and my heart is overflowing with joy.

Cuzco, Peru, February 2023

Detours are the best Tours

F*ck, I get it. Adventure isn't always smooth and comfortable. It gets bumpy and rough at times, and plans fall apart. Itineraries take sudden, different directions, and heavenly experiences can unexpectedly turn into hellish ones. There is always an epiphany to follow, one you didn't expect. You can get the boldness and wisdom of an entire lifetime in just one single day. That day shakes you upside down—you feel the adventure running through each of your cells, and what felt like the worst 48 hours in your life suddenly turns into the heroic experience that makes you grow lifetimes, that makes you feel more alive than one entire city going to work and back home after 20 years of doing the same thing, but I am out here understanding that there is no linearity, and there is no time. Things can suddenly start to swirl and circle like mad, and all you have to do is fasten your seatbelt and suck it up. They denied my exit out from Peru yesterday at the airport because they forgot to give me an entry stamp upon arrival two weeks ago, although I passed through the official checkpoint. (Sometimes, in South America, they ask you if you want to pass through the official or unofficial border.) Sh*t happens, and what had not been my fault could be resolved by neither the police, the central migration office in Lima, nor the German embassy, who were all incapable of helping me because they are too stuck in their bureaucracy and have lost the capability for solution-orientated, flexible thinking as they are controlled by senseless law, order, and power from above, which often turns people into stupid robots, without empathy, addicted to their phones, stuck in the matrix, numbed out, so I had to go and look for a solution by myself instead of staying in the country of Peru forever. I went back more than 1,000 miles to the border checkpoint where I had entered to get the stamp sorted for one ridiculous drop of ink. I travelled by *colectivo*—a mini van or car collecting people on the road—back to Puno, which, whatsoever in South America, means being stuck at road blockages for ages, having to rely on smelly, noisy, dirty *colectivos*, if luckily today, they show up, and to my biggest surprise, I was gifted with a breathtaking drive through the most scenic part of the Andes where tourists hardly go. I will never forget the pictures of the llama herds on deserted plateaus, the flamingos in freezing lagoons, the mesmerizing, majestic Misti Volcano, with its snow top at the horizon towering all, and with my heart and mind opening like never before about the beauty of the planet, and I am floating in bliss on the voyage of my life that I would never want to exchange for any luxury in the world on a holiday with cocktails at the pool in a southern country without excitement, for the sold-up lie of an illusion, for the image of a country that is not true. I prefer real life, and I love adventure. Be brave, my friends. Be free. Be cool.

Somewhere in Peru, February 2023

Like a Thrill

Special, intense, exciting,
At times smooth like a Columbian coffee on a
golden afternoon in the *plaza central* of a sweet
colourful Columbian mountain village,
At other times ecstatic like a Brazilian night
at the edge.
Sometimes I wish this trip,
This thrill,
Would never end.
I take my choices about where to go and what
to do out of moments, from an input I get, a
picture I see, or an encounter I have.
It's like driving high speed fully switched on
taking that Exit 29 you didn't know that existed,
that brings you to
Paradise.

Somewhere in Panama, March 2023

Hidden Paradise

I am in paradise; hidden paradise. Getting here was pure instinct and adventure, as usual. Never seen this place mentioned anywhere before, which is why it is soo cool, and it looks like I am the only tourist here, far away from the few overcrowded, overpriced tourist spots in Panama—I have never understood why people want to go where everyone goes. I can choose between having the beach to myself in front of my house or the main beach where the youngsters hang out and party; it's just that totally amazing Caribbean feel. It seems very chilled here compared to some pretty dodgy places I saw, especially in Panama City; however, I was told that narcotraffic bands are operating all over the country. Nothing to worry about here; I got special protection from the police, and I am being treated by the family where I rent a lovely sea view room facing the white sugar sandy beaches framed by coconut palm trees with the tasty Caribbean cuisine and the freshest fish and boat rides. However, I don't trust anyone, as usual. The policeman asked for my phone number and the hotel of the family where I am staying, which looks wealthy, is empty, although it is high season. Hmm... it's not my business. I'm just swinging in my hammock here, where the only noise I hear is coming from the wind blowing the sea, the loud Latin music coming out of the houses, and the funny parrot noises. Locals here approach me with curiosity and friendliness. Speak their language, and go where no one goes.

La Guaira, Panama, March 2023

Out in the Jungle

I believe that living in the jungle—living in nature as countless Indigenous tribes around the world still do, including in Costa Rica—requires a higher form of intelligence, an elaborated skill of observing your environment, a deep understanding and knowledge of nature and its species, of survival in itself, with a sensible, equal and creative interaction with your natural environment that changes every day in its genius, divine Creation—and living in nature is, in no way, more primitive (as it is falsely commonly advertised) than living a conditioned Western way of life in a little box, doing the same thing every day, which reduces complex intelligence and makes cognitive skills shrink as it requires little creative thinking and acting as we cut ourselves off from our most beautiful, most genius teacher and mother: Mother Nature. And you come back to civilization, and you will dance even more.

Manzanillo, Costa Rica, March 2023

III. Home Land

Back Home

I can't believe I made it back alive, back to organised, tidy Germany—could the contrast be any bigger? No! It's the challenges that make you grow, and after travelling for three months through South and Central America on my own, I feel like a Giant. This trip has been amazing and challenging until the very last minute. I had to face and overcome my own fears and limits many times—nothing feels better once you do—and I was constantly moving outside of my comfort zone. It is what makes me feel alive, where I am most in my element, where life feels like a thrill, and once you've been shaken, you're forever awakened. Adventure is the best addiction in the world! Part of it was that I was ill a few times, had physical challenges due to different climates, heights and diets, squeezed into smelly, dirty, bumpy transports nights and days on the road—that didn't always look like one—into the unknown. I confronted huge jungle creatures, slept in a hundred different beds, ate very delicious and very disgusting things, and I kept walking. I lost flights, have been denied exit, have been taken away personal items and was nearly arrested for disobedience towards authorities. I am still winding myself up like a wild teenager for injustices due to a lack of heart and empathy, for people acting like robots, following harsh rules blindly instead of being human, and I will continue to speak up against it and the harsher the punishment, the more I will love. That is what we are here for—who remembers this? Remembers himself? To remember even more, I will go further and further. I wish to explore the most unexplored corners of the world, the furthest corners of my own soul, and I will find people who look, eat, speak differently and who love the same. I will keep laughing about the system. I will keep teaching what matters and teach the kids not to fear and to have an open mind. I will keep standing up for my rights and beliefs, keep living unlimited adventure, freedom, unity, creativity outside the box, and I will keep writing about it and capturing the beauty of it in shots from around the world. Born to live; born to love.

Ore Mountains, Germany, March 2023

Homeland

Along your journey, you will eventually find that no country is really much better than another in regards to the systems, and most things have good and bad sides, but the country that often frustrates us the most is the one we were born in—but remember it was your own free choice to incarnate there, and this was for a reason. After we roam and see what we learn in different parts of the world, we might eventually come back to our places of birth or another place of soul, and we shall change the things where most needed, create what we want to see instead of searching for it elsewhere. What is fresh and new always seems better, but only at first glance, and you will come to find that the problems we face are similar everywhere in the world and that our dream world doesn't exist unless we create it; this is what we came here for. We can jump in between places and live in different places, which makes life far more exciting, but never miss your here and now. Mother Nature is great everywhere and right where you stand. Water her, respect her, protect her, love her, dance on her. Together, soul family.

Ore Mountains, Germany, December 2022

Huge, Divine, Vast Space

As I am looking through my window, I am counting nine apple—, three cherry—, three plum—, and three pear trees standing in full blossom in our garden. A young orange tiger cat is sneaking through the high grass on her hunt in the golden evening sun. The peaceful silence is only interrupted by some chatting birds. There is a huge, divine, vast space out there for us to fill with sweet, sweet life.

Ore Mountains, Germany, April 2023

Nature, You're My Precious Home

Nature, you're my precious home
My hideaway since I knew how to run
Away from gilded castles and society in a box
Ain't here to paint your box in colours
I go with the river's flow
The wind's blow
Life's grow
In my free world in colours

Ore Mountains, Germany, April 2023

April Rain

April Rain
You washed away my pain
Been sitting on an empty train
Nature looking no more plain
I freed my thoughts from ancient chains
Travel made me free again

Saxony, Germany, April 2023

Community Spirit

A money-based and self-orientated society kills every sense of community spirit. The poorer the people, the bigger the community, is my experience. I have witnessed community in its purest form among the people in South America and Africa, and it is also the place where people seemed the happiest, although owning the least. I know that community spirit does exist in Europe, too, but it is not easy to find in my experience. Sharing and co-creating makes you happier than having it all to yourself isn't a secret. There are a variety of new experimental community forms arising in reaction to a completely missing sense of community in Western cultures. I am talking about New Age circles, or family, as they call themselves, that often separate themselves from the rest by seeing themselves as different or even superior, which is why it puts me off and also because it often takes on forms of another extreme. Can we please remember what true community is about? That it is actually simply caring about your neighbour and being conscious about society as a whole that co-creates and complements each other instead of competes or pleases one another with that strange need to fit in instead of being yourself, unfolding your highest potential for the highest good of all, and instead of chasing blindly after money alone? I believe that we are meant to create a life based on creativity, sustainability, freedom, and independence from the old system based on power and control within our soul tribe, which means nothing more than real friends, people you are on the same wavelength with, connections based on heart and not ego without agenda. The visionaries, those who remember that life is the greatest gift on earth and that we are here to fully live it, not to exist, not to survive, not to function not to buy, but to thrive. Together.

Ore Mountains, Germany, March 2023

Move with the Seasons

Maybe I never settle because I am not meant to settle?! Because I am a true nomad and free spirit at heart, because it does not lie in my nature to imprison myself in a little concrete box and move between the shopping street and work, alone, unhappy, like a slave to the money world, following out orders and duties afraid to fall out of line?! Maybe because my beliefs are as unlimited as the world is, whose borders are artificial and never an obstacle for a true adventurer. Maybe my soul family is scattered all around the world, growing real independent, self-sustainable, happy community lives to jump in between, hop on and off—move with the seasons and how the animals and Native tribes move in alignment with the Universe and the natural flow of life because this is the new yet old, the original template of life?! Maybe I never settled because the world must be explored before I settle. Maybe I never settle in one place because the world is too beautiful to live in one place only, because we are one big, happy tribe of many different traits and colours to complement each other and taste different flavours, scenery and cultures?! Maybe I'm not sitting here with a house, husband, and kids alone because I love all the children of the world and do not need to call one my own. Maybe it is because I will never have this old-fashioned, boring type of relationship, of looking after house and garden, 365 days a year, bound to one place only ever again; that would limit myself, and why would I ever worry how when, what, where instead of just riding that epic wave of life, my friends?!

Ore Mountains, Germany, May 2023

Cosmic Culture

I do not identify with German culture. I do not think that I identify with any culture, in truth. I am really living my own culture, taking the very best out of every culture I have known. Of course, I have been greatly inspired by different cultures and found traits of mine reflected in diverse cultures, but as every manmade concept, culture has its limits, too, but I am unlimited and atypical as I am deprogrammed, meaning free. I love the German straightforwardness, the British eccentricity, the Italian playfulness, the Spanish ease, and the African coolness and so on. However, ways of life don't differ much these days in a world where money is what mostly drives people. Even in the most remote areas with enough open space for a creative mind to come up with a thousand ideas of what to create, people still overwork themselves like robots. How can you be so heavily programmed, I ask myself? It's that money-timetable mentality that gives you four or six weeks of paid holiday from your life, blah blah. I understand that with an awakened mind, it is impossible to follow such a lifestyle. No one is better than another. However, if you are conscious, you see money as nothing more than a byproduct. How could we all forget that it is only just a means to an end? How could you allow it to take the predominant role in your life? How could you become so addicted to materialism? How could you forget what you knew as a child? What is your passion? What will you create? We will find each other and create the new ways together within our soul tribe, and we will create a different currency, a new luxury, some kind of magic.

Ore Mountains, Germany, May 2023

Home II

I am going back home
And nobody can condemn
Me from my land
I chose to incarnate on
Ever again
Because all that I am
Is in plain sight
Not hideable
Ever again
And if it does not fit
Into your fenced-in minds
I shall no more hate
For I am circling above
In my free world
Where I penetrate your walls of fear
With love

Ore Mountains, Germany, May 2023

Free Garden

I have travelled so many different countries and met and lived among so many different nationalities that, instead of becoming like any of them, instead of loving one and hating another, you just become more and more of yourself. You realise that much of what you see in people is cultural programming, not the way people are born—free—and the bigger the picture you get, the wiser and calmer you become. You are an observer. You get inspired or thrilled by some cultures and put off by others according to what matches your character, and you run from that which does not suit you until you realise that all you can ever run from is yourself. You have learned that you can only hate what you engage in and what is a part of yourself until there is nothing left to hate. The way belief systems, social and political systems function and shape people can only frustrate you until you engage in them, but the world is not a country, a government, or a nation that must own you.

These are artificial concepts based on separation and classification and born out of the old power and control energies that can no longer control or disempower you when you understand that the world is a free garden of abundance for you to flourish and dance upon and that you yourself create your own reality at all times by your own beliefs, and that you have the free will to choose what you take part in and what you don't. There is no perfect country, system or nation, but Earth is beautiful and divine everywhere; the rest is our very own Creation. I have asked myself so many times why I chose to incarnate in the country that felt the most unfree to me compared to every other place I have seen, with the Germans seeming so very restricted and stuck in their perfectly organized heads that, consequently, leads to a lack of heart, passion and joy, and I have understood that choosing this land has been one of my greatest challenges in this life, and it is my heart's mission. Home for me has never been the country, the nation or the cultural concept of that place, but nothing but the free land—the energy of the soil, the fields and the woods, the creatures of nature and the mystic, the love, the tradition, and the shelter; the place I call home that knows no frontiers and no limits of freedom and love. And I realize that I love everything else, too, that tried to take away my freedom because this is how I took all of it back, and because it was my dream to show you how to be free, too, as a way shower, a visionary, a pioneer. Out of love.

Ore Mountains, Germany, June 2023

Mother Earth

As a child, my parents and great-grandparents used to take my sister and me out mushroom-hunting in the great big Ore Mountain woods, where we immersed ourselves for hours, not speaking much, becoming a part of the environment, and I remember how much I felt in awe of the big beautiful mystical forest, and I still do the same thing, and it makes me truly happy. Growing up in the former GDR, self-sufficiency was something normal. Almost everybody cultivated a garden and had animals they lived together with. Now the whole permaculture and off-grid movement has become almost trendy in reaction to a consumption-based city life cut off from nature, and I am not keen on one or the other extreme. Living in touch with nature is the most normal thing in the world to me. Also, because I grew up in the country, I guess, where knowing edible plants, berries and mushrooms and living close to animals in the most beautiful playground—the Garden of Eden—which is the reason why I always found parks and playgrounds ridiculous—was normal. Instead of being a visiting tourist in nature, I have always come back to live fully immersed in nature, and I have always observed and learnt from her. She is my greatest inspiration, healer and teacher. Humanity has forgotten that she is the ground you stand on, the food you eat from, the air you breathe in, the house you live in, the calm, and balance you find within. Respect your mother. Mother Earth.

Ore Mountains, Germany, July 2023

Summer

Summer
Heavy you weigh
And I want to talk no more
Trees are whispering
Leaves are weaving
Grass is dancing
In the evening light
Why can't you hear them?
Summer, I love you so

Ore Mountains, Germany, July 2023

Free and Bold

Really proud of myself for having done almost all of my travels on my very own, I started at a very young age to travel abroad, sleeping in my car under the stars and in a thousand different beds, never waited for Prince Charming to carry me around, declined almost every invite to luxury holidays from guys with agendas and worked in a hundred different jobs to afford it. Met many, many special people across the world and experienced f*cking real sh*t and life to the extremes, overcoming my very own fears and limits that made me grow lifetimes, with that adrenaline running through you on that only available taxi that is on the back of a motorcycle, riding through the favelas of Rio with this local lad with these intriguing green eyes to go and see Jesus. Could tell one million stories, and I haven't quite finished yet.

Ore Mountains, Germany, July 2023

IV. East Wards

Starving for Inspiration

I am glad I took another leap of faith right out of my little safe haven, my hidden abundant nature paradise, back home on the country in the East of Germany, with my family and friends that I love to pieces; however, everyone is following the Western lifestyle in the fast lane, living to work, totally blinded by the material world and completely cut off from spirit, and I badly miss real inspiration from people who have integrated a spiritual practice and a work-life balance—happiness—into their daily lives, who study the secrets of the cosmos instead of today's shopping offers and Instagram posts, and who I am eager to find in Central Asia. I feel a vast, divine, open space and smiling people calling me, and I will find them with the compass of my heart.

Mascat, Oman, August 2023

Free Tibet

In one special encounter I had with two Tibetans in Nepal's main buzzing square at the step of one of the numerous stunning temples that is a crazy merge of Kathmandu's hectic daily, with their intriguing spiritual life, I feel I learnt more than some people do in their ashrams and spiritual retreats in weeks, from the most beautiful smile, love and light-heartedness the little Tibetan girl radiated with her dad, giving me a handmade book in the Tibetan language that I cannot read with plenty of Kamasutra paintings inside, and from the mesmerising children's play of the flute that I followed with the highest happy vibes I ever heard into one of the temples. I felt more the soul of the Tibetan culture than I would maybe have on an organised, supervised, expensive tourist-group tour—the only way to get into Tibet—that I decided not to do because the money I'd pay would go to the Chinese government that destroys the Tibetan culture and forced thousands into exile. No matter how hard life is—Nepal is one of the poorest countries in the world—and how unfair and corrupt those who rule the world are, run free and happy like the little Tibetan girl.

Kathmandu, Nepal, August 2023

They Cannot Conquer Holiness

I am lucky that light and running water don't
cut off here in Pokhara in my three-dollar hotel
room where I am at the foot of the 8000 m high
Annapurna range like it did in Kathmandu from
where I came on the worst eight-hour bus trip
of my life, 150 km along the main highway of
the country, and decided to take a flight back to
the capital later, instead, because I don't want
to fall off the unpaved road a hundred meters
down into the riverbed, as it occurs often here.
Why is Nepal one of the poorest countries in
the world despite the million-dollar business of
climbing Mount Everest, which costs between
$40,000 and $100,000 with hundreds of climbs
each week?! Sitting around temples imitating
Buddha isn't enough if we want to stop the
corrupt world leaders. You must stand up and
take your power back, not by conquering the
holy Himalayas, but by standing and acting in
your sacred power from within. I am at the foot

of the sacred Machhapuchre, which is one of the very few peaks that cannot be climbed. They cannot conquer holiness.

Pokhara, Nepal, September 2023

Wake up to Your True Power

To me, holidays are a break from the hamster wheel, a break from your life they make you pay hard for, but life is more about than being on and off duty. Life is about self-realisation, and a true voyage is a spiritual journey of self and world discovery for your growth and inspiration on the path of Oneness while you learn more than they could ever teach you. Self-realisation is living your purpose whatever your gifts, talents and passions may be, and money is a byproduct of that, nothing but a means to an end instead of the primary focus within a work-life balance—don't forget to smile, meditate, chant, pray, walk, eat, breathe, love in tune with Mother Earth and all forms of life instead of self-destruction. The lady I am staying with in the Nepalese mountains is getting the corn, tea and tomatoes from her garden out to dry in the sun. I am reflecting the Western trauma while gazing at the wonders of the world, the peaks of the Himalayas from my room that costs five dollars a day, while other people believe they could never afford a Nepalese holiday, as they charge you thousands of dollars for an organized trip. Follow the program or wake up to your true power.

Annapurna, Himalaya, Nepal, September 2023

Himalaya

Himalaya
Standing in your sacred power,
Deeply rooted in the mother with your
crown in the heavens
You don't fight to be in your right
Standing in your sacred presence
That reminds me of who I Am
Om Namah Shivaya
Himalaya

Annapurna, Himalaya, Nepal, September 2003

My Nomad Heart is Beating Faster

My Nomad Heart is beating faster since I set my foot on Mongolian soil. Ever since, my heart has been aching for living under the great blue skies of the endless land in tune with the elements, the seasons, the animals, the natural flow of life; an old love, indeed. All my life, I have been the happiest outside, beyond little concrete boxes, walls and frames. Nowhere do you feel freer than waking up in a traditional *ger* (yurt) with dozens of eagles circling above you, to the freshest air I ever breathed, and flying on the back of a wild Mongolian horse over the endless serene, beautiful grasslands. To me, this is one of the most inspiring places I ever travelled to, also because it is the least Westernised and globalised country I have ever witnessed. The Mongolian people have maintained their very own proud, strong individual and independent identity, and they are the sweetest and coolest folks I ever met. They are incredibly hospitable, friendly, open-minded and smart due to their way of life and due to the fact that they apply their own critical mind instead of being programmed by the media and social norms and constraints. They don't look poor at all but rather wealthy, and they dress up kind of cool—you see them in those long, colourful satin coats with a belt and a hat and sunglasses, riding those vintage motorbikes. I am in the former capital of the huge, vast, ancient Mongolian Empire. I only figured it out when I visited the most special Buddhist Erdene Zuu Monastery that dates back to the 16th century, and I am staying in a yurt I rent from a lovely local family whose kids seem super mature, independent and smart and who look after the whole place by themselves when their dad just goes out into the wild for days—something completely normal in Mongolia. The country has only three million inhabitants, of which one-third live a nomadic life, and the towns have a handful of shops only where they sell the locally produced products and that what is needed instead of overconsumption and waste. The nomad way of life is, in truth, the most sustainable, responsible, conscious, natural and happy way of life there is, the opposite of an archaic colonial Western way of thinking to be superior, and it is the future. Owning little, having all. Freedom.

Kharkhorin, Mongolia, September 2023

Balanced Way

I am really proud of myself that I have found a way to travel the world with little money that saved me from falling into the common tourist traps, where an image of a country is sold that has little to do with reality. I know that people go on holidays to get a break from their ordinary lives, so the cocktail and pool might work, but I live a life I don't need a break from, and I travel for adventure, inspiration, and to broaden my views. I am always looking for the local experience, and this is how I get treated like a local, which truly touches my heart when I notice strangers caring about me and welcoming me with open arms, which I have experienced so many times around the world, especially in places where true community still matters more than money. To truly get to know foreign places, you need to mingle with the locals, and that just happens by itself here in Mongolia, as the people are so heartful and open-minded, and that originates from their nomadic travelling tribes and lifestyle—nothing opens your heart and mind more. I have been hugged by the sweetest kids, invited into homes, shared meals, exchanged so many smiles and communicated with sign language, and most importantly, with the language of the heart that everybody understands. Never have I seen such open-minded, friendly, free and happy kids. I believe all children are by nature, but the upbringing and education turn many kids into fearful, intimidated or even nasty ones. Here, you see them all playing outside together, and they automatically smile at you when they see you, whereas they would look away where I come from. Here, they came running to me with their huge, curious hearts. They fed me with pine nuts, took shots with my Nikon, hugged me, and didn't stop chatting to me, although I understood nothing except 'Where are your mom and dad?' Growing up in nature, community and around animals has major positive effects on children. The children being so incredibly careless, lighthearted, joyful and free, touched me deeply and reminded me to do the same, to go out and play and have fun and not take life so seriously. I have also noticed the healthy, light, spiritual practice of the Mongolian people—not as an extreme religious programming as I have observed in other countries, but a natural way—I call it light or healthy Buddhism, and I realized how we share the same beliefs without me ever studying it in books but by discovering its great universal truths, by following the path of the heart and through the discovery of myself and the world. Seeing people in Asia singing mantras or dancing on the pavement, speaking to their Gods while cooking or sitting meditating in the streets and squares, is the most normal thing, whereas you would be judged crazy if you did the same in the West. It is truly time for everyone to understand the great spirit and cosmic laws if you want to spend less money on booze, pills and psychologists. Mongolia, especially, inspires me because I notice how people here still apply their common sense, opposite of so much programming in the Western world where people just follow blindly the matrix, whereas here, life feels natural, full of sense and soul. Genuine.

Kharkhorin, Mongolia, September 2023

Ride into the Unknown

Yesterday, I hired a local on a motorbike to take me out to the mountain by just pointing in the direction of the horizon behind the sand dunes that looked intriguing to me, and it's not a good idea to walk as everything that looks close in Mongolia is very far away. We communicated in sign language, and I gave him $10, for this is the way I learned to travel like a local for the real deal, out of the initial reason of never having much money, and that has saved me from falling into the main tourist traps where I learned to be brave and apply common sense by observing my environment and listening to my intuition,—that is better than any paid guide in the world and the best guarantee for adventure and to get to know a country as it really is instead of some fake, sold up tourist image, plus, it gave me the opportunity to learn, grow and expand myself in the broadest ways instead of ticking off tourist sites from a list other people consider important! My driver brought me to the most special, hidden place of incredible, pristine energy, where the monks had erected some small Buddhist temples, for they recognized the mountain as holy. On my ride through the free, vast, open grasslands, I passed by a few nomads'yurts and camels and many sheep and goats, with my friendly driver singing some songs, me thinking I could live here, *lol*. The one who will overcome the fear of the unknown will be gifted with the greatest freedom, fun, and magic.

Kharkhorin, Mongolia, September 2023

Land of Freedom

Mongolia
My heart was aching for the land of freedom
That I recognized
By the burning flame inside of me
That was lit like never before
When I saw the endless steppe and grasslands
Shimmering in the golden light again
Where only the horizon calls my name
Where we sit under a million stars
around the fire
Share our hearts
The eternal love
For the land of freedom
Forever burning

Kharkhorin, Mongolia, September 2023

Once, I was a Shaman

I know that
In another life
I was a shaman
Somewhere between the magical
Mongolian steppe
And the deep forests of Siberia
I could fly with the eagles, run with the horses,
dance with the spirits
I could do anything
Now, I cut all cords and chains that keep
humanity entangled
The old towers of power and control are falling
New Earth is blooming, and all her children are
running free again

Kharkhorin, Mongolia, September 2023

Nomad by Nature

I thought I would slow down with travelling next year, but how can you ever stop once you've really tasted Freedom? What mostly inspires me around the world are genuinely friendly, positive, and open-minded people, and I have connected with so many warm-hearted people on my travels around the world and very much here in Mongolia, where they made me a part of themselves, inviting me to sit and eat with them by the side of the road when they saw me waiting for a bus in the middle of nowhere, brought me to the other side of the city of Ulan Bator in person when I asked for directions, and all of the other sweet encounters I will never forget. They will share everything with you where capitalism and egoism haven't spoiled the hearts. Although I look different from them, here they don't judge you by your looks but recognize you as a traveller they welcome with open arms, and there is no intention behind their actions other than compassion and love, very much the opposite of the culture I was born into, and out of that reason, I never wish to live there full time. Just go and stay like a nomad in his yurt on the free land when and wherever he is guided by nature, intuition and wisdom.

Kharkhorin, Mongolia, September 2023

Soul of Siberia

Holy breeze
Carrying the golden leaves of joyful birch trees
Sparkling the carpet of soft sands
Washed on your shores
From your crystal pure waters
From the depth of your soul
Where I dance alone
With the spirits
In fairytale, light-flooded woods of larch and
pine
Holy Baikal
Here and beyond
Glorious Creation
Celebration

Maksimikha, Lake Baikal, Siberia, Russia, October 2023

Hitchhiked to Goryachinsk

Hitchhiked to Goryachinsk, Lake Baikal, East shore, where the Trans-Siberian Railway doesn't spit out any foreign Baikal tourists who don't come any more, but I am all alone, together with the few locals. It doesn't get any more real than this. I'd better leave the jewellery in the room. The camera, too. You never know. You learn this when you travel the world alone: don't take that kind of risk. Others, you do take. Like going to Russia when the call is stronger than the fear they try to spread. Travelling alone in Siberia is safer than any big city in my home country, Germany, and you lose the fear by travelling around the world on your own. More and more, you trust in your own intuition and become strong on your path and soft in your heart. Wherever you go, people are kind to you because you are, and you feel infinitely free. Every day brings a new discovery about yourself and the world. Lake Baikal, the deepest, oldest and purest lake in the world, is a miracle—you have to experience her in her wisdom and power, surrounded by dense, endless taiga woods, and Siberia is Siberian. Magical and lonely. There is more vodka than fresh food; they eat buckwheat instead of rice, the houses are made of wood, the tablecloths are crocheted and the people think I am Russian until I speak. If it's not cosy, it's bleak. An interplay like life itself. Many people move to the city until they understand that life there is even lonelier than in Siberia if you don't join hands—don't fall into the capitalist's trap. Lenin's idea of social justice was good, but he didn't bear in mind that it cannot be dictated from above but rises from below, from the deep understanding from within that we are all equal and that the real power lies in your own hearts and hands, and when you see the beauty instead of the hopelessness of your Siberian village, your freedom is your independence. Everyone here knows that the war is a business of the powers that be, but they have no power if you don't give them the power.

Turka, Lake Baikal, Siberia, Russia, October 2023

Freedom

Everybody can sit at a hotel bar and order a cocktail but not everybody can handle remoteness. You, alone in a place nobody wants to go because nobody ever mentioned it in a tourist guide. People are like sheep. Follow the herd blindly, but I am like a lone wolf who follows her instincts to discover the world and choose her herd well. The city person lands on a bus in the beauty of the wilderness, and their first remark will be: there is nothing. The wolf understands that nothing is everything. He hears the elements speak, the wind, the waves, the trees, the other animals, and sits quietly and listens to the nothing that reveals the magic, the secrets to the one who listens beyond time. Silence speaks. He needs no fence around him to feel safe, but he loves to roam in space. He trusts he'll meet a friend like himself.

Turka, Lake Baikal, Siberia, Russia, October 2023

Shamanic Ritual

In Asia, it is completely normal to witness spiritual practice in everyday life. You see people outside singing their mantras, going into meditation anywhere in public, standing next to the highway in deep prayer with a bowl of milk, or you become a part of a shamanic ritual like I did today. A group of friends from the local Buryat tribe, who have a very strong shamanic tradition, waved me over as I went for a stroll through the woods along the shore of Lake Baikal when they saw me sitting on a rock, listening to their drumming. I was given *chai* and snacks to eat. Lake Baikal and the spirits were worshipped through singing and gifted with vodka, huge cakes, cigarettes, clothes, tea and more. The shaman—shaman by birth and just a normal girl, not some self-declared narcissist expensive, Western guru speaking to the nature spirits—went into a trance and channelled spirit and blessed every one in the group. I was naturally made a part of the ceremony, no matter my background, origin or beliefs, just because I happened to be there, guided by spirit as always, of course. It was a dream come true. I am very drawn to this type of culture because it combines spirit with nature and creativity, such as music and dance. Soo much more beautiful than sitting in a church being made a sinner. It is beautiful and touching to see people sharing their religion with you and talking to spirit and their Gods in everyday life. If I did anything similar in public in Germany, I would be judged crazy in a culture that has completely cut itself off from spirit and has forgotten its true nature as a part of All. Dance, prayer, nature, expression, community. Human cosmic nature.

Turka, Lake Baikal, Siberia, Russia, October 2023

Spiritual Masterclass

This Asia trip isn't just one of the greatest adventures, immersing myself in the most diverse cultures that inspire and broaden my horizon in the most enlightening ways; it is a spiritual masterclass. On the one hand, there is Tokyo, where I felt as if I was in an apocalyptic film—the matrix, with its seeming robot-like people moving in perfect order between an endless sea of grey skyscrapers—and then there is the other Japan, a different reality that tastes real, with its lush mountains and Feng Shui. There is the Daosim and the Qi energy I am tuning in. There are so many different teachings in this world, and I observe how many students become dedicated pupils, slaves to a doctrine, whether they are the Buddhist monks or the *new age hippies*. In my eyes, spiritual practice often takes on too extreme forms. It is nothing that requires to be lived, per se, but to be applied in normal, everyday life, I believe. For me, this is really not about one belief system or the other giving it its absolute righteousness. These are the limits of belief systems that come with the narcissistic need to be righteous, and if any teaching wants to see you as a dedicated follower, it is no more wise but disempowering, controlling. Instead of becoming a follower of one or another belief system, I have studied the secrets of life through inward and outward observation of myself and on my travels around the world, and I have received very much knowledge and wisdom that I mostly picked up energetically and through observation instead of being a follower of someone who wants to be right, and I am thrilled at what I receive. Nor will I convert to Hinduism, Buddhism or Daosim as I haven't to Protestantism or become a *new age hippie* but integrated many different aspects because I am either one or the other, but all of that what has greatly inspired and thrilled me because they are parts of my own cosmic soul. Places can carry energy that is information coming from the light or landscapes, and then there are places of the matrix, without energy, like big cities, with the people moving like robots in a scheme that feels like an apocalyptic film, and then there is this dream. This other reality. Heaven on earth. I can channel the wisdom and knowledge from the trees, from the energy of a place, from the music or temples or rocks, which all have an energy imprint you can pick up, rather than becoming a student of a thousand books that others wrote. I read thousands of pages during my studies at university, and now I write my own books that are not about me but written for you to remember yourself.

Oshino Hakkai, Japan, October 2023

Fujiyama

Silver bamboo blossom fields glow in the
distance at your foot
You hide your white snow crest in the
clouds today
I couldn't find the way
So I cycled out and lay in a meadow by a stream
There was a bridge
With bamboo blossoms on the other side
I walked across
And you were very close to me
Fujiyama
You blew the clouds away

Oshino Hakkai, Japan, October 2023

Apocalyptic Show

Tokyo
You lock your entrance-fee-parks at night and
carry your people in buses out on Sundays to
visit fenced-in nature to throw coins into shrines
and hunt souvenirs.
It's trendy to walk around like a copy of a fake
comic king or queen.
Your trees are speaking louder, the dragons are
laughing and your mountain ranges are rising
above your skyscrapers.
Your future feels apocalyptic, baby!

Tokyo, Japan, October 2023

Tam Coc Heroine

Eat like a local, which means Vietnamese noodle soup for breakfast, because you will be greatly disappointed by any copy of Western food made just for international tourists in this part of the world; no, I am none of them! You will find most of them grouped up in the same ho(s)tels, restaurants and activity spots, following online reviews and recommendations, staring at their phones while crossing the street. I wonder how many get overrun by the flood of motorcycles—no step without Google Maps; never without the phone, but you forgot how to make a phone call. The hero/heroine is not the Instagrammer from the Banana Tree Swimming Pool hotel but the boat-rowing Vietnamese lady who rows together with the others hundreds of tourists every day to a once-upon-a-time beautiful spot in nature that has been sucked out—a type of non-integrative, non-sustainable, profit-based tourism—I call it neo-colonialism—that I don't support. No, this is not

Vietnam! The old charm of it still exists; I found it in the smiles of the people and in the nature and corners where no one looks at, and while you chase up the bus for your next destination on your itinerary or Buddhist temple, I am lying here in the sunshine, surrounded by the beautiful Tam Coc rocks, gazing at the falling leaves, flowers and butterflies, experiencing the Buddhist way to be that is in every Now. Don't be a follower. Be a leader. A leader of the heart.

Tam Coc, Vietnam, October 2023

She Holds the Key

My beautiful, gentle, innocent, pure Vietnam—
I have come to see your soul and love you on my
last day after you taught me all the hard lessons
I needed to learn. Now I am feeling like a queen,
rolling in my luxury bed that is, in truth, a bus, but
it matters no more through your green, tropical,
banana, coconut palm tree and bamboo garden,
and I am free, free-floating, finally free from all
the burden and pain of the old world, free at last.
This voyage ain't definitely no sightseeing—it
is spiritual evolution, a growth together in love.
There are so many ebbs and flows, tales to tell,
challenges you face, bridges you cross, epiphanies
you have and precious souls you meet along
your way. After all, you realize that all that ever
counted was that moment, and that is all that
you have. Good or bad, embrace it, live it without
judgement or overthinking. Just live it. And there
she stands. Little beautiful girl holding the key.

Sapa, Vietnam, November 2023

Landing in India

Landing in India after ten weeks in Asia deep-dive feels sooo good!! Like a celebration. My taxi threw me out somewhere in the crazy centre of Varanasi, where I got a ride on a motorcycle down to the steps of the Ganges River—the holiest site in India—where you can see the dead bodies burning and the pilgrims bathing in the river that has that goose bump atmosphere with all of the temples, ceremonies, candles and boats. Feeling very welcomed by the lovely locals who told me helping is good for karma—they love to show you the way through the buzzing labyrinth of a thousand bazaars, rickshaws, bikes, motorcycles and people—and hash is good for Kamasutra, *lol*. Although they take their beliefs very seriously here, there is joy in the air, and I don't feel the need to cover up at all, and less at 30 degrees, as I was told you have to in India. No argument in the world justifies the need for a woman having to cover up and a man not, and you'll earn more respect for being who you really are than by a declaration of other people's beliefs and stigmas. Long or short dress, the lords truly don't care.

Varanasi, India, November 2023

I am the Master Manifester of my Dreams

I am the master manifester of my dreams. This means that you must paint out your wishes of the heart precisely and very clearly and without a single doubt of receiving them because why would you not be given that of which you dream, and then you give it away to the Universe, and it will be given to you. This is what I did. I longed for a place in Goa without any noise, without hoards of *new age hippies* or tourists in a beautiful, cool house under palm trees with a great bed and a terrace facing the ocean, and this is exactly what I got. It just showed up to me today while I walked along the beach—actually, a fisherman brought me there after we had a chat at his hut under the palm trees by the ocean between the fishing boats and flowers that I love so much with the locals that love to share their meals with me and treat me like family. I did not want to stay in a small, half-moon palm tree bay overloaded with a hundred sunbeds, beach shacks, hotels, people with a thousand stories and with that noisy animation for people who cannot handle silence, cannot handle life, cannot handle themselves, who need a constant program, who have zero understanding of nature, but all I hear from my room is the sound of the ocean. I needed to listen to the earth and the cosmos again. My greatest inspiration. Here it is, just me and the fishermen—who often give me dinner straight out of the boat—and the wide, open, warm, enchanting, powerful, beautiful Indian Ocean. I needed to be by the ocean. The ocean is my animation, healing my soul, cleansing my body, filling me up with power, with life.

Colva, Goa, India, November 2023

Born Again

And it is after 18 countries, you've travelled on three continents only just this year, a great mission you've been pushed on and that was facilitated by the forces of the Universe following the compass of your heart, after the 18 lives you've lived in just one year after a deep dive into all of the diverse cultures, dimensions and times, there is the sudden moment of completion, and joy starts penetrating each of your cells, and it is reflected in the children's play and laughter, in your dance at night time on your terrace to the beat of the nearby beach club under coconut palm trees in the ocean breeze in your bikini, reflected in the fishing boats that make a drawing, dipping into the red Indian sunset together out at sea, a joy and light-heartedness you've missed and never want to miss ever again and that you will carry with you wherever you go. You are born again. It is in the moment you release all of the old beliefs that life is hard and difficult when you unlock the cosmic flow of love and life that you feel running through your body. The moment you know you create your own dream in each instant, you create whatever you dream of, the moment you flow. Keep on riding the cosmic wave of love and life that is always there to hop on, my friends.

Colva, Goa, India, November 2023

Bombay Love

I am glad that I didn't have the money to stay in the legendary Taj Mahal Palace Hotel, where the money spent in just one day could lift out all of India from poverty but that I kissed you in an old, run-down, red, Colonial, five-storey hotel opposite the Taj Mahal, leaning against the window under the full moon rising, gazing at the warm, free, golden Indian evening sky here in Bombay. Only love can make you real. Makes you walk through the gate from illusion into reality, from the shadow into the light. Makes you become again what you have always been. Love.

Bombay, India, November 2023

Life is a Dream, and You are the Author

About the Author

Janet Kaufmann was born in the former GDR in the East of Germany, where she witnessed the Berlin Wall coming down as a child. She studied and graduated in Education, Psychology and Foreign Languages at the University of Leipzig in Germany and at the University Aix-Marseille in France. Besides German, she speaks fluent English, French, Spanish and Italian. She has been working as a schoolteacher and private teacher in Germany, Russia, Italy and Hungary as well as a journalist for the international department of the German MDR television and the French ARTE televison among many other different jobs in Germany, France, Spain, Monaco, England, Scotland and more to gain life experience and to afford her travels.

She has written three books in the five languages that she speaks—*Age of Liberation* published in 2021, *Taste of Freedom / L'Esprit de Liberté / Sabor a Libertad* published in 2023 and *Like a Thrill / Wie ein*

Rausch / Alla corrente del vento published in 2024. In her books, she shares how she broke free from limiting beliefs and the norms and constraints of society and culture on her leap of faith that took her around the globe, experiencing many different countries and cultures. She shows us how to reach an inner state of freedom, love and unity consciousness and inspires and encourages us to live a new template of life based on freedom, independence, creativity, and community with a holistic approach other than living a conditioned life in a little box. Her books come with unique adventures, inspiration and empowering messages to create the new ways of life together by stepping out of the old program of fear, control and power from above. She shows us how we can rise, stand in our power and create a self-determined happy life and a new, better world together.

She has travelled since a young age to almost 60 countries in Europe, North- and South America, Africa and Asia. Besides her travels around the world, the author now lives between Germany and India and engages in different, self-sustainable and creative projects with the local community, friends and family worldwide. As an artist, she shows her extraordinary photography from around the world in different places and galleries. She just turned her first own short film in India. She wishes to inspire the world and engage in positive change through her literature and arts and her free and happy way of life.

In the Fire of Our Love
The old ways and world burnt down to the ashes
Sprinkled in the holy waters
Where we Rise
As a New Cosmic Order
Of Divine Love

Wie ein Rausch

Schriften aus der ganzen Welt,
die deinen Horizont erleuchten

Janet Kaufmann

Die einzige Revolution, die stattfinden kann, ist
die aus dem Inneren unserer Herzen.

Inhaltsverzeichnis

I. Nord Wind

Ich bin eine Künstlerin

Ich bin eine Künstlerin
Ich brauche viel Ruhe
Damit sich mein Geist erholt in seinem Schiff
Auf dieser physischen Erde
Auf die wir kamen
Um wieder zu lieben

Insel Skye, Schottland, Oktober 2022

Tick Tack Tock

Tick Tack Tock
Schafft alle Uhren ab
Zeit im Rahmen
Passt nicht zu meinem Namen
Erde und Himmel sind mein Kompass
Sonne und Mondlicht
Leuchten meinen Weg
Lebe Tag für Tag

Insel Skye, Schottland, September 2022

Reden, reden, reden

Reden, reden, reden
Oh, all der Leute ihr Gerede
Sinnloses Geschnatter
Wetter, Nachbar, Premierminister
Noch ein Bier, Geschnatter ohne Angst
Nächster Morgen
Schweigende Stille
Wo ist deine Aktion?
Doofe Ablenkung
Egal, das Wetter
Bauen wir die Welt besser

Insel Skye, Schottland, September 2022

Wanderseelen

Wir, die Wanderseelen, reisen nicht nur zum Spaß allein—es ist viel mehr als das. Was für dich vielleicht wie Urlaub aussieht, ist tatsächlich auch Arbeit. Während die anderen in Büros sitzen oder Supermarktregale auffüllen, restaurieren und reinigen wir verzerrte Energien von ganzen Ländern und Völkern, verbinden Orte, Zeiten und Dimensionen und verankern kosmisches Bewusstsein, während wir in unsere eigene Unbegrenztheit expandieren, in Liebe und Einheit mit allem, was ist und abends gehe ich dann manchmal noch in den örtlichen Pub arbeiten. Also nicht so anders als du, und ich habe auch die Supermarktregale und Bürojobs gemacht, aber keine menschliche Versklavung mehr für mich, nein! Wir mögen über unseren kosmischen Job nicht so viel sprechen, und das meiste machen wir unbewusst, und du machst das vielleicht auch, oder weißt du, wohin du nachts in deinen Träumen gehst?

Insel Skye, Schottland, September 2022

Nasser, kalter, blauer Ozean

Vor meinen Augen ein nasser, kalter, blauer Ozean. Heute kurze Wellen, ein Schlagen und Klatschen auf die großen runden Kieselsteine vor dem Kai. Klatsch, Klatsch. Der Strand ist fast untergetaucht. Das Meer ist heute gekräuselt und wiegt ein paar Fischerboote. Kleine und große, blaue, gelbe, rote, grüne, braune Fischerboote. Manche schwanken so stark, dass einem fast schwindelig wird. Einige kommen rein, andere fahren raus. Ich frage mich, was sie wohl für einen Fisch gefangen haben. Ich will mitfahren. Vielleicht treffe ich den Fischer. Ich laufe einer steifen Brise auf dem Kai entgegen. Keine Seele weit und breit an diesem kalten November Montagabend. Schwache Lichter kommen aus den bunten Häusern, die sich entlang des Kai aufreihen. Alle sind zu Hause. Ich bin der einzige Zuschauer im Kino heute.

Insel Skye, Schottland, November 2022

Der Fischer

Die Magie dieses kleinen Ortes—es gibt sie noch, und du wirst sie finden, wenn du nicht zu einer der Touristenattraktionen eilst. So sitze ich hier an diesem kleinen felsigen Strand, an dem sich die Touristen meist nicht verirren, während sie Fotos vom Pier aus machen und die anderen im Pub sitzen und trinken und so habe ich ihn ganz für mich allein, mit den Seevögeln die ein- und auftauchen und dem sanften Brechen der Wellen die eine Handvoll Fischerboote schaukeln gesäumt von den bunten Fassaden—das pinke, blaue, grüne und gelbe Häuschen, von denen jedes seine eigene Geschichte zu erzählen hat und so treffe ich den Fischer, der an diesem wunderschönen Oktobertag auf seinem Boot hinaus fährt.

Insel Skye, Schottland, Oktober 2022

Regenbogenbrücke

Im Leben geht es ganz um Improvisation, Anpassung an den immer gegenwärtigen Moment, der sich in einer Million Möglichkeiten entfaltet. Es ist gut, fest zu sitzen. Es ist großartig, nicht mein Auto zu haben. Diese leere Straße entlangzulaufen. An einem kalten, aber atemberaubenden Novembertag. Den ersten Schnee auf den Bergkuppen zu sehen. Die Erde unter meinen Füßen zu spüren. Wie die Energie durch meinen Körper rennt. Die frische Brise auf meinen Wangen. Die Schafe am Straßenrand grüßend. Meinen Atem langsamer werdend zu spüren, weil ich in der Natur bin, in Ehrfurcht vor der Schöpfung, durch die Regenbogenbrücke laufend. Das Gefängnis der Gesellschaft wird zu einem unsichtbaren Tropfen irgendwo hinter dem Horizont. Es ist wundervoll, von diesen netten Kroaten, Ukrainern, schottischen Einheimischen und Reisenden mitgenommen zu werden und die Aufregung des Lebens zu teilen. Es ist großartig, aus diesem Auto wieder auszusteigen, mich umzudrehen, die Wolken hereinkommen zu sehen, ihnen vorweg zu laufen, in das Licht. Durch den Regen, in die Dunkelheit. Zurück ins Licht. Immer zurück ins Licht.

Insel Skye, Schottland, November 2022

Spirituelles Erwachen

Ich muss ungefähr 16 gewesen sein, als ich zum ersten Mal die andere Welt entdeckte und liebte, die unphysikalische Welt. Wir sind tatsächlich immer darin als Babys und Kinder. Ich erinnere mich daran, wie ich von zu Hause wegrannte, um auf einem eingeschneiten Hügel auf meinem Rücken zu liegen, in einer weißen Wüste in den Himmel schauend und an einer Zigarette ziehend, von der mir schwindelig wurde—ein Zustand, den ich irgendwie mochte, denn er löste mich von der physikalischen Welt, der Welt, die ich kannte. Die Menschen nehmen Drogen und trinken Alkohol, um sich für eine kleine Weile von ihrer schmerzhaften physischen Existenz zu befreien, die schmerzhaft ist, wenn wir uns vom Geist abtrennen, von der Quelle, von der Natur, von unserem wahren Selbst, von dem, was wir wirklich sind. Früher habe ich es auch mit dem Gras und den Drinks übertrieben, weil ich nicht genug davon bekommen konnte, an diesem Ort zu sein, wo ich einen größeren Sinn spürte, eine Tiefe, die in unseren physischen, programmierten täglichen Leben, fehlte—ein Ort, wo ich mich mehr zu Hause fühlte, bis glücklicherweise in meinen Dreißigern mein höheres Selbst entschied, ein spirituelles Erwachen zu haben, anstatt an einem Rock-n'-Roll Leben zu sterben, was mich schlagartig dahin katapultierte, wo ich hingehörte—auf meinen Seelenweg, auf eine sehr heftige und extreme Weise, was der Bruch war, den ich brauchte. Im technischen Sinne öffnete es meine Chakren, mein drittes Auge, um zu Sehen und all die anderen Chakren, mit der größten Lebensenergie durch mich rauschend—Kundalini-Energie, kosmische Energie. Eine Öffnung und Aktivierung meiner Energiezentren—das ist alles, was ein spirituelles Erwachen wirklich ist und es ist an der Zeit dies klarzustellen—es ist eine Öffnung deiner Chakren, die dich wieder mit der Quelle verbinden, mit der Natur, dem Kosmos, mit deinem wahren Selbst und nichts würde jemals wieder wie zuvor sein und niemals wieder wirst du Drogen und Drinks brauchen, denn jetzt kannst du immer an diesem heiligen Ort sein auf natürliche Art und mit ein bisschen regelmäßiger, spiritueller Praxis wie Meditation, Introspektion, Ausdruck Deiner Seele, Erdung in der Natur, Vermeidung von allem, was Toxisch ist, und auch dort bleiben—so einfach. Jetzt habe ich den Faden verloren, was ich eigentlich sagen wollte, was ist, warum ich Dinge liebe, die sich ein bisschen kosmisch anfühlen und schmecken neben den erdhaften Dingen, die ich genauso liebe—sie sind in der Tat miteinander verbunden und ich möchte gern die Bedeutung der Verbindung beider unterstreichen im täglichen Leben und in der Gesellschaft, welche fehlt, weswegen die Welt außer Balance ist. Deswegen preise ich Freiheit und tiefe Liebe. Deswegen liebe ich unbegrenztes Reisen und episches

Abenteuer, einfach leben. Einfach das Leben leben außerhalb von dieser doofen kleinen Kartonschachtel, in die sie dich hineinstecken wollen, und ich hatte niemals die Absicht, sie nicht zu durchbrechen.

Insel Skye, Schottland, Oktober 2022

Neue Schule

Als Lehrerin von Beruf glaube ich nicht mehr an unser Schulsystem und ich habe große Zweifel daran, ob ich mich in dieser Form je wieder engagieren möchte. Ich glaube, dass Lernen natürlich passieren muss, ohne zu starre Stundenpläne, Mauern und Rahmen, und durch Entdeckung und Erkundung anstelle von Indoktrinierung, um Kinder zu erziehen, die in der Lage sind, für sich selbst zu denken, eine Meinung zu bilden und eine Zukunft zu bauen und Wege zu finden, sich selbst zu realisieren und um glücklich zu sein. Das neue Lernen könnte in Form einer Gemeinschaft stattfinden, wo die Erwachsenen und Älteren mit den Kindern ihr Wissen teilen, ihre verschiedenen Fähigkeiten und Begabungen und Talente, was alles Mögliche sein kann, vom Gärtnern, Tanzen, Singen, Bauen, Zeichnen, Meditieren, Reiten, Kochen usw., was von den Erwachsenen in ihrem täglichen Leben ausgeführt wird, anstatt in einem Job zu arbeiten, um nur ihre Rechnungen zu zahlen. Auf diese Weise, wird der Lernprozess natürlich und bereitet mehr Spaß in allen unterschiedlichen Altersgruppen und Gemeinschaft baut Werte wie Liebe, Respekt, Einfühlungsvermögen, Integrität und Zusammensein auf, anstelle von Ego-getriebenen, miteinander wettstreitenden und unsicheren jungen Leuten und unglückliche Erwachsene. Es muss Zugang und direkte Interaktion mit verschiedenen Interessensfeldern für die Kinder geben, wie Kunst, Literatur, Philosophie, Fremdsprachen und Kultur, Geschichte, Botanik usw. welche die Kinder selbst auswählen und studieren können, allein oder zusammen, anstatt steifen Lehrplänen zu folgen, die vor viel zu langer Zeit von Menschen aufgestellt wurden, die überhaupt keine Ahnung vom echten Leben haben, und anstatt unter einem ständigen Leistungszwang zu stehen. Sie müssen viel Raum haben, um gar nichts zu tun oder was immer sie wollen, weil so die großartigen Ideen geboren werden,

und weil wir geboren wurden, um frei zu sein.
Das Schulsystem ist veraltet, wenn du auch ein
Visionär bist, wenn du dich traust, frei zu sein.

Insel Skye, Schottland, November 2022

Sieh ihr Herz, wenn du deines öffnest

Lass dich von den unfreundlichen Menschen nicht beirren, die dich nicht mögen, weil du glücklich bist. Und lass dich davon niemals abbringen, andere glücklich zu machen. Wie der Whiskey Trinker der mir gesagt hat, dass er mich liebt und wie schön es war, ihn lächeln zu sehen als ich heute Vormittag an der Bar stand, einfach so weil ich mich niemals von allen unterschiedlichen Menschen abgrenzen darf, sondern mitten im Leben stehen will und weil mein Kollege in der Küche genauso erleuchtet sein kann, wie derjenige, der es offen deklariert und ich darf nicht darüber urteilen, wer und was ich selbst nicht bin, sondern muss die Gleichheit unserer Herzen sehen, anstatt der oberflächlichen Unterschiede und ich muss alle zusammen bringen, das ist das was ich liebe. Wie der junge Mann, der heute vergeblich am gleichen Ort wie ich zu trampen versuchte und natürlich habe ich ihn eingeladen mitzukommen, bei meinem Fahrer der anhielt und wie er sich freute, dass der

Fahrer genau dorthin fuhr, wohin er den ganzen Tag versuchte hin zu kommen — ihn glücklich zu sehen, machte mich glücklich und der Fahrer war ebenso glücklich, weil er heute mit noch niemand gesprochen hatte und glücklich war auch mein irischer Freund, mit dem ich heute spazieren ging und der schottische Freund, den ich morgen treffe — sich gegenseitig glücklich machen, egal, woran du glaubst, woher du kommst, was du machst und zu sehen, dass wir alle eine große Familie sind, ist das Schönste, was ich vor allem auf meinen Reisen gelernt habe, indem ich in alle möglichen unterschiedlichen Welten und Kulturen eingetaucht bin und es gibt immer eine Möglichkeit jemanden glücklich zu machen, einfach irgendeinen Fremden der auch da draußen auf der Straße ist so wie du und urteile niemals jemanden anhand seines Äußeren, sondern sieh ihr Herz, wenn Du deines öffnest.

Insel Skye, November, Schottland 2022

Steck' deine Liebe in etwas Größeres

Wir können so viele Dinge lieben. Meinen Nachbarn, die Katze meines Nachbarn, meine Mutter, deine Tochter, meinen Freund, den Fremden auf der Straße, der mein Lächeln erwidert. Wir können Frauen, Männer, Kinder und Ältere, Tiere und Pflanzen, Steine, die Sterne, die Sonne, den Regen, den Wind lieben. Was wir lieben, ist ein Teil von uns selbst. Ich fühle die Liebe für den Wind und den Kosmos in jeder einzelnen Zelle meines Körpers. Es macht mich größer, als ich bin. Liebe expandiert. Muss ich Sex haben mit dem, was ich liebe? Ja und nein. Sex könnte diese Verbindung verändern, diese Freundschaft. Liebe ist ätherisch und Sex ist physisch, und ja, wir können beides verbinden, aber nur, wenn da Liebe ist. Wenn es abhängig macht, dann ist die Liebe nicht mehr frei oder sollten wir die Liebe einfach fließen lassen? Es gibt so viele verschiedene Stadien und Tiefen von Liebe, und ich glaube, dass man es fließen und verschmelzen lassen muss und man zusammen aufsteigt, wenn es wahre Liebe ist. Wenn es freundschaftliche Liebe ist, glaube ich, ist es nicht wert sie auf körperlicher Ebene zu teilen—dieses immer während zur Konfusion führende Thema, das zu offenen Beziehungen führt, Betrug und Lügen, oder hast du von einer Hippiekommune gehört, wie in den 70ern die für immer glücklich war? Wenn man *high* ist, ist es vielleicht cool, aber am nächsten Tag sieht es anders aus. Warum überhaupt eine Beziehung haben, wenn man gleichzeitig andere Partner will? Warum können wir dann nicht einfach Freunde sein? Ist das dann nicht eine Co-Abhängigkeit, weder in der Lage, mit oder ohne einander zu sein? Ich glaube, es gibt endlose Formen, Liebe zu leben, auch in weiblich-männlichen Freundschaften, die wir ausbauen können. Etwas zusammen erschaffen. Steck' deine Liebe in etwas Größeres.

Insel Skye, Schottland, November 2022

Halloween-Party

Sorry, ich komme nicht auf deine
Halloween-Party
Ich finde, du siehst komisch aus
Ich finde es nicht lustig
Ich liege nachts wach und *downloade* Gedichte
Und du denkst, ich bin komisch
Es ist nicht lustig
Wir tragen nur Namen
Die Sterne kennen dich besser

Insel Skye, Schottland, November 202

Zwischen Welten

Nur eines der unzählbaren Dinge, die ich gelernt habe auf meinen Reisen durch viele verschiedene Länder, Jahre und Erfahrungen, ist, dass das Ziehen von Ort zu Ort in meiner Natur liegt, und wenn ich mich jemals niederlassen sollte, wird es nur für ein paar Monate sein, bis ich zu meinem nächsten Ort oder zu meinem nächsten Abenteuer weiterziehe, anstatt mein Haus zu meinem Gefängnis zu machen, kontrolliert durch die materielle Welt, anstatt immer mehr Dinge, die ich im Leben nicht brauche, anzusammeln und zu konsumieren, oder anstatt dick und faul in meinen Routinen und Komfort Zonen zu werden. Wenn ich mich niederlassen würde, wäre es niemals wieder in einer kleinen Betonschachtel, da ich, sobald ich meine Augen öffne, mit meinen Füßen auf die Mutter Erde treten, den Horizont sehen und in die Sonne laufen, möchte. Ich habe auch gelernt, dass wenn die Leute dich nicht integrieren oder Türen sich für dich nicht öffnen, dort, wo du lebst, oder wenn du keine echten Freundschaften geschlossen hast, es an der Zeit ist, weiterzugehen. Wie auch immer, wird kein Ort auf der Erde dein Zuhause jemals ersetzen, die Wahl deiner Inkarnation, dein Boden, dort, wo du geboren wurdest und aufgezogen. Das bedeutet nicht, dass wir für immer an diesen Ort gebunden sein müssen, denn wahre Liebe kennt keine Anhaftung, nicht an Menschen, nicht an Orte, nicht an Dinge. Wir können an verschiedenen Orten leben und sie genießen, anders als uns die Gesellschaft vorgibt, ein Gefangener unseres Jobs, Hauses, Besitzes, unserer Kreise, Pläne und der Zeit und des Ortes in einem Rahmen, zu sein. Ein veraltetes Konzept, das nur zu jemandem passt, der wirklich niemals Freiheit geschmeckt hat.

Insel Skye, Schottland, November 2022

Mein launisches, schönes Schottland

Mein launisches, schönes Schottland
Jetzt bleibt uns nicht mehr viel Zeit
Süße Melancholie des einsamen Nordens
Durch dich habe ich in die tiefsten Ecken meiner
Seele geschaut
Deine raue, zerklüftete Schönheit
Hat mich in den dunkelsten Tagen getröstet
Für die Mutigen
Um das Licht zu finden

Insel Skye, Schottland, Dezember 2022

Rüttelnder, lauter Bus

Ich lege meinen müden Körper auf die hinteren
vier Sitze schlafen
Schaue an mir vorüberziehenden,
schneebedeckten Bergketten, mit einem
weißen Himmel verschmelzend, zu
Trag mich, trag mich weit fort
Rüttelnder, lauter Bus wiegt mich in den Schlaf
Ich werde an einem anderen Ort aufwachen
Mit einem neuen Leben
Reite die Wellen weiter

Insel Skye, Schottland, Dezember 2022

II. West Wärts

Rio, Downtown!

Ich höre der wunderschönen Klaviermusik vom unteren Stockwerk zu, die ein Konzert im Takt mit dem warmen Regen, der auf meine Terrasse tropft, spielt, während ich in meinem Bett im Hotel Americano liege, welches überhaupt nicht amerikanisch, sondern sehr brasilianisch ist, und die tausend farbenfrohen Bilder des Tages schießen durch meinen Kopf wie ein Rausch, einfach wie der Tag ein glückseliger Rausch war. Mein erster Tag in Brasilien, in Rio de Janeiro, und im Gegensatz zu den Stimmen der anderen und des amerikanischen Touristen an der Rezeption, der sagte, Rio sei gefährlich und dass sie dich sofort ausrauben, stürzte ich mich in die Straßen, in die Flut, in das Feuerwerk, in das pralle Leben. Nicht im weltbekannten Copacabana oder Ipanema Bezirk, wo ich mein Hotel in letzter Minute absagte, sondern im wahren *Downtown*, wo die Leute von Rio de Janeiro leben. *Oh Jesus, que bênção foi ser pobre!* Ich lief in den Straßen und spürte keine Gefahr, im Gegensatz zur

Warnung des Amerikaners, an der Rezeption, der glaubt, er sei besser als die Brasilianer, und nur weil er die Leute ausraubt—er arbeitet in den Finanzen—bedeutet das nicht, dass ich auch ausgeraubt werden muss! Jeder kreiert seine eigene Erfahrung! Ich habe sie gesehen, die Rio de Janeiro Leute, und sie haben mir zugelächelt und ich fühlte mich willkommen—wunderschöne Menschen, freundliche Menschen—ich habe ihr Herz gesehen und sie haben meins berührt. Da ist so viel Schönheit in der Mischung der indigenen, afrikanischen und europäischen Kultur auf diesem Kontinent, und sie erscheinen leicht im Herzen, und aus jeder Ecke kommt Musik. Samba, Reggaeton und andere großartige, laute Musik und ich habe geniale Straßenkunst gesehen. Ich bin in der Altstadt, im Herzen der Stadt mit all den Straßenparties—viele Menschen schlafen hier auch auf der Straße und es gibt viele Armut- und Drogenprobleme. Ich habe die Schüsse aus den Favelas gehört, aber so ist das Leben—besser als in einer Seifenblase zu leben und an einer langweiligen Bar mit Touristen in einem versnobten Copacabana Hotel zu sitzen. Ich bin lieber hier, mitten im Leben, mit den Menschen, ich liebe sie alle! Ich werde mir auch Ipanema und Copacabana anschauen und ich werde sie auch lieben, ganz so wie die Brasilianer ihre Strände lieben und morgen steige ich auf den Zuckerberg und jetzt muss ich schlafen, mit meinem kleinen Edelstein Toukan, der mich freundlich anlächelt und der mich faszinierte, als ich ihn auf dem Straßenmarkt sah—der Regenwald ruft mich auch! Das Abenteuer vor meiner Haustür! Ich bin in Südamerika und ich könnte nicht glücklicher sein!

Rio de Janeiro, Brasilien, Januar 2023

Rio Rausch

Vier Tage in Rio fühlen sich so an wie ein ganzes Leben irgendwo anders auf der Welt! Ich bin so verliebt in diese schönste Stadt der Welt und in ihre Menschen, ihren Lebensstil, ihre Lebensfreude, Verrücktheit, ihre Kontraste und „Oh mein Gott", in Ihre Musik! Samba, Bossa Nova, Reggae..! Das Leben hier passiert einfach auf der Straße und alles ist eine Improvisation oder ein Abenteuer, und obwohl ich müde sein müsste, fühle ich mich energiegeladen. Obwohl ich das Stadtleben eigentlich nicht mag, fühlt es sich hier anders an—als ob sie alle zusammenhalten würden als eine große Familie in diesem verrückten Leben. Die Leute machen einfach ein Feuer mitten auf der Straße, um etwas in einer Konservenbüchse zu kochen und essen auf dem Bürgersteig, warum nicht! Sie verkaufen hier die besten Caipirinhas an jeder Straßenecke und sie kosten nur 50 Cent! Da ich keinen Alkohol mag, trinke ich immer Kokosnusswasser direkt aus einer Kokosnuss und ich esse Unmengen an exotischen Früchten, seit ich hier bin—ich hab' schon etwas an Gewicht verloren—man tanzt hier einfach viel und das Leben fühlt sich generell so leicht an, tatsächlich fühlt sich jeder Tag wie eine Party an! Ich wollte gerade ins Bett gehen, aber die Trommeln auf der Straße sind so laut, dass ich einfach nicht widerstehen kann.

Rio de Janeiro, Brasilien, Januar 2023

Brasilien

Hmm Brasilien
Ich werde mich an dich erinnern durch den
Geruch deines köstlichen Kaffees, der nach
grünen, satten Bergen in tausend Grünnuancen,
die mit dem smaragdfarbenen Meer
verschmelzen, schmeckt
Durch deine wundervolle Mischung glücklicher
Menschen in allen Farben
Durch deinen Samba, Bossa Nova und Sertanejo
Durch deine exotischen Früchte und Blumen
Durch dein in den Bann ziehendes Trommeln
Von Menschen, die vor langer Zeit in hölzernen
Booten von weit her kamen
Durch deine überschwängliche Fülle
Durch deine Verrücktheit
Durch deine *Beleza*
Durch dein großes, kostbares Herz

Costa Verde, Brasilien, Januar 2023

Wind, trag mich fort

So hing ich mit einigen Einheimischen in diesem Hippie-Vibe-Dorf ab, die mich zu einem Teil ihrer täglichen *asados* — südamerikanische Grill- und Musik-Sessions machten im Haus von El Barba — 84-jähriger Poet und revolutionärer Künstler, wo sich Freigeister treffen und ihre Ideen über die Welt austauschen und viel Tango, Fado, Murga, Candombe, Choclo, Son, Salsa, Bossa Nova... . Was für ein Genuss! Jetzt lass' ich mich weitertreiben vom Wind. Sei wild und frei wie ein uruguayisches Pferd.

Rocha, Uruguay, Januar 2023

Uruguay

Und ich lernte zu fließen
Gracias Uruguay
País del Río de los pajaros pintados
River river
Water water
Mar y Sol
Jetzt fließen

Rocha, Uruguay, Januar 2023

El Camino

Ich habe mich diesem äußerst genialen Weg hingegeben, der bisher größten Reise meines Lebens durch Südamerika, allein. Vom ersten Teil in Brasilien, der sich großartig, aber etwas holprig anfühlte mit der tropischen Hitze, vielen Moskitos, dem Lärm, einer kranken und vielen kurzen Nächten und mit meinem Telefon, das vom Boot auf den Grund des smaragdfarbenen Meeres fiel und dass nach 24 Stunden von einem einheimischen Taucher wiedergefunden wurde, von dem man sagt, er würde alles finden—ohne Ausrüstung natürlich—und mit meinen geretteten Britischen und Deutschen SIM Karten—aber die Botschaft war klar—so hat sich die Reise in einen genialen Ritt gewandelt, intensiv und schnell, mit vielen unvorhersehbaren *Moves* und Abenteuern die hohen Wellen zu surfen lernend was dir diesen *Thrill* gibt—was dich daran erinnert, wie sich das Leben meistens anfühlen sollte—wie eine Ekstase und nicht wie ein Schlaf oder wie ein

Kampf. In dem Moment, wo ich all meine Pläne aufgab und aufhörte, das Internet auf meinem Telefon zu benutzen, um Orte zu finden, wo ich schlafen oder als nächstes hingehen könnte—in dem Moment, wo ich mich dem *Flow* hingab—öffneten sich überall, wo ich hingehe, Türen mit besonderen Begegnungen und Verbindungen auf meinem Weg, die mich von einem Ort zum nächsten führen—ein Schritt führt zum nächsten—geniales, aber oft ignoriertes Prinzip des Lebens, nichts als den völligen Moment zu umarmen ohne Erwartungen und ohne zu viele Pläne. Auf diese Weise öffnete sich der Weg—*el camino*—von ganz allein, indem ich ihn laufe. Geniales universelles Prinzip nicht nur dieser Reise, sondern des Lebens, das sich in seiner Magie entfaltet, wenn wir wenig Erwartungen haben und den Moment leben. Auf diese Weise bin ich in meinem Traumhäuschen gelandet, wo ich derzeit bin, das fast nichts kostet in der *Sierra de Cordoba*, im Herzen von

Argentinien—das wahre, echte Argentinien. Kein Tourist weit und breit, die währenddessen alle in das teure und touristische Patagonien strömen. Sie haben hier immer noch diese altmodischen Tante-Emma-Läden wo sie das Essen in kleine Mengen selbst abpacken, und alles ist organisch und super lecker hier. In jedem Geschäft, in das ich kam, begannen die Leute ein Gespräch mit mir—sie sind unglaublich freundlich und herzlich hier—das ganze Gegenteil von dem, wie ich die *Porteños* kennenlernte—die Leute von Buenos Aires. Es ist wunderbar, den Geist der Gemeinschaft und das Leben in seiner Einfachheit, aber Schönheit zu sehen, wenn der Kapitalismus die Gesellschaft noch nicht ganz durchdrungen hat und nicht die guten Dinge im Leben verdorben hat—wenn Liebe und Zusammensein die Menschen antreiben, anstelle von Gier und Egoismus. Die Leute hier sehen wirklich glücklich aus und das Ausgehen und die Musik spielen eine große Rolle im täglichen Leben überall und ständig in Südamerika. Die Läden schließen um Mitternacht und die Argentinier gehen wirklich spät ins Bett, und wie in Uruguay fahren sie hier diese coolen alten Autos, und sie lieben es, ihren *Mate*—Getränk der Einheimischen aus Kräutern—miteinander zu trinken, der ein großer Teil der argentinischen Identität ist. Das Häuschen, in dem ich zurzeit bin, befindet sich inmitten unberührter Natur und sitzt auf dem ältesten Fels der Erde—ja, er reicht sogar bis in das Haus hinein—ich kann ihn von meinem Bett aus berühren, da mein neuer Freund Marcos, der ein cooler Typ ist, der die Welt selbst bereist hat, bevor er diesen kleinen Hafen hier baute, den er mit Besuchern teilt, den Geist der Landschaft integrierte. Es sitzt auf einem unterirdischen Bach, welcher dir lebhafte, bunte Träume gibt, sagt er. Der große, wilde Fluss ist einen kleinen Spaziergang entfernt, wo die Einheimischen baden, und der die Landschaft mit wunderschönen Becken, worin man schwimmen kann, und sogar mit Stränden, geformt hat. Alles, was ich nachts höre, sind die Vögel und das Konzert der Grillen, während ich in den atemberaubenden Sternenhimmel schaue—Natur—zurück gehen woher wir kommen, wo sich alles reich und göttlich anfühlt, jenseits der Illusion von Zeit.

Mina Clavero, Argentinien, Januar 2023

Frei ziehen

Ich würde gern für immer um die Welt ziehen. Ich liebe die Bewegung, den Wechsel der Landschaft, der Eigenarten der Menschen und Kulturen, den Wechsel des Essens, der Flora, der Fauna und des Klimas. Das Lächeln und die offenen Herzen der Menschen bleiben gleich, wo auch immer ich hingehe. Ich liebe es, Flüssen zu folgen, durch Täler und Bergketten, die sich zum Meer hinstrecken, Ozeane zu durchqueren, von Insel zu Insel zu hüpfen jenseits des Unbekannten. Manchmal bleibe ich an einem Ort hängen, aus einem Grund. Reflektiere mich selbst und den Weg und blicke die Sterne etwas länger an. Werde ich ein Raumschiff sehen?

Irgendwo in Argentinien, Januar 2023

Eine Welt

Wer auch immer das war, der mir sagte, das Fremde zu fürchten, das Weite, das Andere, das Unbekannte, war ein Lügner. Deine Welt ist meine Welt und meine Welt ist deine Welt. Nichts ist schöner als mein Mittagessen heute in dieser öffentlichen Küche in der Stadt mit den Einheimischen, den Kindern, den Älteren, den Reisenden zu teilen—einer dieser besonderen Momente des Reisens. Ich aß die beste Titicaca-See-Forelle der Welt. Sie essen hier sehr gut, vergolden ihre Zähne, ziehen sich richtig gut an und sind wirklich süß, aber sie nennen Bolivien ein Dritte-Welt-Land, weil sie das Geld nur in ihren eigenen Ar*ch blasen. Sieh, wer glücklicher ist. Je mehr ich reise, desto mehr fühle ich mich als Teil des Ganzen. Distanz und Unterschiede sind nur eine Illusion der räumlichen Welt, die jemand Ängstliches erfand. Nicht in meiner Welt. Unserer Welt. Die Leute hier behandeln mich überhaupt nicht anders, weil ich in ihnen niemand Anderes sehe. Ich sehe Schönheit. Ich sehe Liebe. Ich bin mit wenig Geld gereist, ohne mir einen Kopf darüber zu machen, wie viel übrig bleibt—sich Sorgen zu machen, ist auch für die Ängstlichen. Reisen macht dich reich im Inneren. Für immer.

Copacabana, Titicaca See, Bolivien, Februar 2023

Welten verbinden

Machu Picchu war seit Monaten geschlossen und sogar peruanische Reiseführer sagten mir erst vor zwei Wochen, dass er auf unbestimmte Zeit geschlossen sei und dass das Reisen in Peru wegen politischen Unruhen nicht möglich wäre—man sagte, er würde vor April nicht öffnen. Ich habe keine einzige Demonstration gesehen und sie haben Machu Picchu überraschenderweise vor zwei Tagen wieder eröffnet, als ich ein Ticket kaufte, die normalerweise Monate vorher ausverkauft sind, und ich hatte Machu Picchu so ziemlich für mich allein. Wenn ich auf andere gehört hätte, wäre ich niemals nach Peru gekommen. Jedoch habe ich anstatt dessen auf meine Intuition gehört, die mir sagte, einfach loszugehen, und meine Reise über den Titicacasee und durch die Berge war leicht und besonders, als wenn sie begünstigt worden wäre—ja, so war/ist der ganze Trip in Südamerika, warum? Weil ich meinem Herzen gefolgt bin und sich so Türen öffnen. Warum möchten so viele Menschen Machu Picchu besuchen? Um es auf ihrer Liste abzuhaken? Ich hasse diesen Ausdruck—macht auch ein wirklich gutes Foto daneben zu posieren. Warum kam ich nach Machu Picchu? Nun, weil ich den Ruf hörte. Welten und Dimensionen verbinden. Ich bin kein Tourist, ich bin eine Reisende, eine Entdeckerin und ich bin ein Kind des Kosmos—das wir alle sind—ob du dich daran erinnerst oder nicht.

Machu Picchu, Peru, Februar 2023

Kosmisches Wunder

Mist! Warum würde ich ausgerechnet einen Tag vor meiner Besteigung des Machu Picchu krank werden, mit Durchfall, weil ich diese verlockende, exotische, mir unbekannte, gelbe Frucht aus dem Regenwald aß, die gut für die „Reinigung des Körpers" ist—Durchfall, um es beim Namen zu nennen, hat man mir später erklärt! Also besteige ich natürlich dennoch Machu Picchu, nachdem ich 10000 Meilen überwunden hatte, um hierherzukommen—ziemlich erschöpft und müde aufgrund der magischen, gelben Frucht und ich werde ganz emotional, als ich mich der Stätte nähere—wegen meines physischen Zustandes oder ist es Machu Picchu, der mich überwältigt? Erstaunt wandere ich durch die Stätte, gehe an kleinen Touristengruppen vorbei, die von Unmengen an Informationen von ihrem Touristenführer bombardiert werden und denke mir, dass ich all diese Information niemals aufnehmen könnte, also hänge ich etwas beim zentralen Sonnentempel umher—hier fühle ich etwas Starkes und Faszinierendes—nach einer Weile gehe ich weiter, aber ich komme zurück und bleibe noch etwas länger an dem besonderen Ort bis einer der Wächter mich bemerkt und fragt, ob ich im rituellen Schamanentempel meditieren möchte, der dem Sonnentempel gegenüber steht und für Touristen normalerweise nicht zugänglich ist, und überhitzt von der Inkasonne, ist es genau der Ort wo ich sein muss, also führt er mich heimlich in den geheimen Tempel wo ich im Schatten der riesigen Steinblöcke sitze und mein Körper fühlt sich erleichtert an und ich beginne zu atmen, atmen, atmen und da passiert es: mein Bewusstsein öffnet sich den höheren Dimensionen und den unteren und allen Dimensionen und allen Zeiten—die Vergangenheit und die Zukunft sind jetzt hier. Ich empfange die kosmischen Energien und Geheimnisse durch mein Kronen-Chakra, in meinen Körper bis zur Wurzel in die Erde hinein und umgekehrt—von meiner Wurzel hoch in den Himmel und ich verbinde gestern, heute, morgen und für immer. Dies ist der Beginn des Neuen Zeitalters. Es ist hier und jetzt. Ich bin jeder Moment.

Machu Picchu, Peru, Februar 2023

Bürger der Welt

Du wechselst dein Zuhause alle paar Tage oder Wochen. Genauso wie das, was du isst, das mit den Orten, die du bereist, wechselt. Du isst Früchte und andere seltsame Dinge, die du noch nie zuvor sahst. Es ist dir egal, ob du manchmal deinen Instant-Kaffee kalt trinkst, mit deinen Händen auf dem Bett isst, weil du keinen Tisch hast, und es gefällt dir, weil du dich frei fühlst, während du aus deinem Fenster deines kleinen, süßen Gasthauses schaust, das dich viel weniger kostet als ein Haus zu Hause zu mieten, und du schaust auf die Hügel und den Slogan—*Viva el Peru*—der dort steht. während die Sonne langsam und friedlich über den roten Dächern von Cuzco untergeht und die fühlst dich wie ein Bürger der Welt. Du bist dir nicht sicher, ob du jetzt aufhören solltest—manchmal wünschst du, dass dieser Trip nie zu Ende geht—du könntest für immer weiter und weiter gehen, jedes mal mutiger, weiser, ruhiger und glücklicher und du weißt, dass dein Körper manchmal müde wird und du lässt ihn müde sein—du eilst nicht umher nur dann, wenn du musst und du weißt wann du dich zusammenreißen musst und wenn du manchmal rennen musst, dann wirst du rennen und wenn du trotzdem den einzigen Bus verpasst, sagst du dir, sch**ß drauf, und es gefällt dir, gestrandet zu sein und du weißt nicht genau, was besser ist—die Aufregung der Bewegung—die sich ändernden Landschaften, Höhen, Klimata, Vegetationen und Züge und Bräuche der Menschen anzuschauen oder an einem Platz länger zu bleiben, der dir vertraut wird und dessen Geheimnisse du bei einem tieferen Blick entdeckst, aber du weißt, dass es genial ist, das Leben. Und deine größte Sorge, wenn du darüber nachdenkst, was du heute anziehst, ist, über rot oder grün zu entscheiden, weil alles, was du brauchst, in einen kleinen Rucksack passt, und wenn etwas fehlt, dann kaufst du es einfach auf der Straße und wenn dein Lieblingshut vom Wind auf dem Schiff, auf dem du bist, weggeblasen wird, lässt du ihn gehen und schenkst ihn dem silbernen Meer des

Rio de la Plata und du glaubst fest daran, dass du einen noch Besseren finden wirst. Und den neuen Hut, den du in Bolivien kaufst, lässt du zurück für denjenigen, der ihn in Peru finden wird, weil er zu deinem Stil in Kolumbien nicht mehr passt, und du wirst sogar einen noch cooleren in Panama finden. Und manchmal findest du neue Freunde auf deinem Weg und du verabschiedest sie wieder, und du weißt nicht, ob du sie jemals wieder siehst, aber du weißt genau, dass du sie für immer lieben wirst.

Cuzco, Peru, Februar 2023

Cuzco

Diese Reise fühlt sich so genial an, weil sie nicht in Zeit oder in irgendwelchen anderen Glaubenssätzen begrenzt ist. Die Welt ist mein Wohnzimmer. Manchmal fühle ich mich, als würde ich fliegen—wie der südamerikanische Kondor, der hoch oben zur peruanischen Flöte, die im Hintergrund spielt, kreist, und mein Herz fließt über vor Freude.

Cuzco, Peru, Februar 2023

Umwege sind die besten Wege

Mist, ich hab's kapiert. Abenteuer ist nicht immer einfach und bequem. Manchmal wird es holprig und schwierig und Pläne zerfallen im Nichts. Routen nehmen plötzlich neue Richtungen, und himmlische Erfahrungen können auf einmal unerwartet zu höllischen werden. Danach folgt immer ein Durchbruch, einer, den du nicht erwartet hattest. Du kannst den Mut und die Weisheit eines ganzen Lebens an nur einem Tag bekommen. Dieser Tag wird dich durchschütteln—du fühlst, wie das Abenteuer durch jede einzelne deiner Zellen rast, und was sich wie die schrecklichsten 48 Stunden deines Lebens anfühlte, kann sich plötzlich in die heldenhafte Erfahrung wandeln, die dich um ganze Leben wachsen lässt—die dich lebendiger fühlen lässt als eine gesamte Stadt, die jeden Tag zur Arbeit trabt, die seit 20 Jahren das Gleiche macht, aber ich bin hier draußen und ich verstehe, dass es keine Linearität und keine Zeit gibt. Dinge können wie verrückt zu kreisen und zu drehen beginnen, und alles, was du tun musst, ist dich anzuschnallen und die Zähne zusammenzubeißen. Gestern haben sie mich am Flughafen nicht aus Peru herausgelassen, weil sie vor zwei Wochen vergaßen, mir einen Stempel im Pass bei der Einreise zu geben, obwohl ich durch die offizielle Grenzkontrolle kam. (Manchmal fragen sie dich in Südamerika, ob du durch die offizielle oder inoffizielle Grenze willst.) *Sh*t happens* und was nicht mein Fehler war, konnte auch nicht von der Polizei, der zentralen Einwanderungsbehörde in Lima und der deutschen Botschaft gelöst werden, die alle nicht in der Lage waren, mir zu helfen, weil sie zu tief in ihrer Bürokratie feststecken und die Fähigkeit, lösungsorientiert und flexibel zu denken, verloren haben, da sie zu stark von sinnlosen Gesetzen kontrolliert werden—von Ordnung und Macht, wodurch viele Leute zu unempathischen, dummen Robotern werden, abhängig von ihren Telefonen, verloren und ohnmächtig in der Matrix, und somit musste ich mir allein eine Lösung ausdenken, anstatt für immer im Land Peru zu bleiben. Ich ging über 1000 Meilen zurück zu der Grenze, wo ich hereinkam, um einen Stempel zu bekommen, für einen lächerlichen Tropfen Tinte. Ich reiste im *colectivo* — einem Minibus oder Auto, welches die Leute auf der Straße aufsammelt — zurück nach Puno, was wie auch immer in Südamerika bedeutet, für eine Ewigkeit an Straßensperren stecken zu bleiben und auf schmutzige, laute, stinkende *colectivos* angewiesen zu sein, falls sie heute überhaupt auftauchen, und zu meiner größten Überraschung wurde ich mit der atemberaubendsten Fahrt durch den landschaftlich schönsten Teil der Anden beschenkt, wohin Touristen fast nie kommen. Ich werde niemals die Bilder von Lamaherden auf einsamen Hochplateaus vergessen, Flamingos in eiskalten Lagunen, den majestätischen, in den Bann ziehenden Misti Vulkan, der mit seiner Schneekuppe alles überragt und wie mein Herz und mein Geist sich wie nie zuvor über die Schönheit des Planeten öffneten, und ich schwebe im Glück auf der Reise meines Lebens, die ich niemals für irgendeine Luxusreise der Welt oder einen Urlaub mit Cocktail am Pool in einem südlichen Land ohne Aufregung eintauschen würde, für eine verkaufte Lüge einer Illusion, für ein Bild eines Landes, was so nicht stimmt. Ich bevorzuge das wahre Leben und ich liebe das Abenteuer. Seid mutig, meine Freunde. Seid frei. Seid cool.

Irgendwo in Peru, Februar 2023

Wie ein Rausch

Besonders, intensiv, aufregend,
Manchmal sanft wie ein kolumbianischer
Kaffee an einem goldenen Nachmittag auf dem
zentralen Platz eines süßen, bunten Ortes in
den kolumbianischen Bergen,
Ein anderes Mal, extatisch wie am Rande einer
brasilianischen Nacht.
Manchmal wünschte ich diese Reise,
Dieser Rausch,
Würde niemals zu Ende gehen.
Ich treffe meine Entscheidungen, wohin ich
gehe und was ich tue in Momenten, von einer
Eingebung, die ich bekomme, einem Bild, was
ich sehe oder einer Begegnung, die ich habe.
Es ist, als würde ich *high speed* fahren, völlig im
Flow und diese Ausfahrt 29 nehmen, von der ich
nicht wusste, dass es sie gibt und die dich
ins Paradies bringt.

Irgendwo in Panama, März 2023

Verstecktes Paradies

Ich bin im Paradies, im versteckten Paradies. Hierherzukommen war purer Instinkt und Abenteuer, wie immer. Hab' diesen Ort nie irgendwo erwähnt gesehen, weswegen er so cool ist, und es sieht so aus, als wäre ich die einzige Touristin hier, weit weg von den wenigen überfüllten, überteuerten Touristenorten in Panama—ich habe nie verstanden, warum die Leute dort hingehen wollen, wo alle hingehen. Ich kann hier zwischen einem Strand für mich allein vor meinem Haus oder dem Hauptstrand, wo die Jugendlichen abhängen und feiern, wählen—es ist einfach dieses total geniale Karibik Feeling. Es kommt mir hier ganz gechillt vor, verglichen mit einigen zwielichtigen Orten, die ich sah, vor allem in Panama Stadt. Wie auch immer, mir wurde gesagt, dass Drogenbanden überall im Land agieren. Hier gibt es keinen Grund zur Sorge. Ich habe persönlichen Schutz von der Polizei und ich werde von der Familie, wo ich ein hübsches Meerblickzimmer am von Kokosnusspalmen gesäumten, weißen Puderzuckerstand miete, mit köstlicher karibischer Küche und mit dem frischesten Fisch und Bootsausflügen verwöhnt—jedoch vertraue ich niemandem wie immer. Der Polizist fragte mich nach meiner Telefonnummer, und das Hotel der Familie, wo ich bin, sieht wohlhabend aus, obwohl es leer steht und obwohl Hauptsaison ist. Hmm... mir egal. Ich schaukele einfach in meiner Hängematte hier, wo das einzige Geräusch vom Wind, der das Meer bläst, von lauter Latino Musik aus den Häusern und lustigen Papageienlauten, kommt. Die Einheimischen hier nähern sich mir mit Neugierde und Freundlichkeit. Sprich ihre Sprache und gehe dort hin, wo niemand hingeht.

La Guaiara, Panama, März 2023

Draußen im Dschungel

Ich glaube, dass im Dschungel zu leben—in der Natur zu leben—so wie es immer noch unzählige Naturvölker auf der ganzen Welt tun wie auch in Costa Rica—eine höhere Form von Intelligenz verlangt—eine hoch entwickelte Fähigkeit deine Umwelt zu beobachten, ein tiefes Verständnis und Wissen über die Natur und ihrer Spezies, des reinen Überlebens mit einer sinnvollen, ausgewogenen und kreativen Interaktion mit deiner natürlichen Umwelt, die sich jeden Tag ändert in ihrer genialen göttlichen Kreation—und das Leben in der Natur ist in keinster Weise primitiver, als es fälschlicherweise hingestellt wird, als das konditionierte westliche Leben in einer kleinen Box, wo man jeden Tag dasselbe tut, was zu einem Schrumpfen komplexer Intelligenz und kognitiver Fähigkeiten führt, da es kaum kreatives Denken und Handeln verlangt, wenn wir uns von unserem schönsten und genialsten Lehrer, von unserer Mutter, Mutter Natur, abtrennen. Und du kommst zurück in die Zivilisation und du wirst noch mehr tanzen.

Manzanillo, Costa Rica, März 2023

III. Heimat Land

Zurück Daheim

Ich kann nicht glauben, dass ich wieder zuhause bin, lebendig—wieder im organisierten, sauberen Deutschland—könnte der Kontrast größer sein? Nein! Es sind die Herausforderungen, die dich wachsen lassen, und nachdem ich für drei Monate allein durch Süd-und Mittelamerika gereist bin, fühle ich mich wie ein Riese. Dieser Trip war bis zur letzten Minute genial und herausfordernd zugleich. Ich musste meine eigenen Ängste und Grenzen viele Male konfrontieren und überwältigen—Nichts fühlt sich besser an, wenn du es schaffst—und ich habe mich ständig außerhalb meiner Komfortzone bewegt. Das ist das, was mich lebendig fühlen lässt, wo ich am meisten in meinem Element bin, wo das Leben sich wie ein Rausch anfühlt, und wenn du einmal geschüttelt worden bist, bist du für immer wachgerüttelt. Abenteuer ist die beste Droge der Welt! Dazu gehörte, dass ich ein paar Mal krank wurde, körperliche Herausforderungen aufgrund von verschiedenen Klimata, Höhenmetern und Lebensmitteln, eingequetscht in enge, schmutzige, rüttelnde Transporte—die nicht immer danach aussahen—Tag und Nacht auf der Straße ins Unbekannte. Ich habe riesige Dschungekreaturen konfrontiert, in einhundert verschiedenen Betten geschlafen, habe sehr leckere und sehr eklige Dinge gegessen und ich lief weiter. Ich habe Flüge verloren, wurde an der Ausreise gehindert, mir wurden persönliche Dinge entnommen und ich wurde fast verhaftet wegen Ungehörigkeit gegenüber Autoritäten. Ich rege mich immer noch auf wie ein wilder Teenager wegen Ungerechtigkeit, wenn Herz und Empathie fehlen, über Leute, die sich wie Roboter verhalten und harschen Regeln blindlings folgen, anstatt menschlich zu sein, und ich werde weiter aussprechen, was ich denke, und je härter die Bestrafung ist, desto mehr werde ich lieben—deswegen sind wir hier, wer erinnert sich daran? Wer erinnert sich an sich selbst? Um mich noch besser zu erinnern, werde ich weiter und weiter gehen—ich möchte die unerforschtesten Ecken dieser Welt erkunden, die meiner eigenen Seele, und ich werde Menschen treffen, die anders aussehen, anders essen und sprechen, und die genauso lieben. Ich werde weiterhin über das System lachen, werde weiter das lehren, was zählt, und ich werde den Kindern lernen, keine Angst zu haben und einen offenen Verstand zu haben. Ich werde weiterhin für meine Rechte und meinen Glauben einstehen, weiter grenzenloses Abenteuer, Freiheit, Einheit, Kreativität außerhalb der Box leben, und ich werde weiter darüber schreiben und die Schönheit der Welt einfangen in Fotos aus der ganzen Welt. Geboren, um zu leben, geboren, um zu lieben.

Erzgebirge, Deutschland, März 2023

Heimatland

Entlang deines Weges wirst du schließlich herausfinden, dass kein Land wirklich besser als ein anderes ist hinsichtlich des Systems, und die meisten Sachen haben gute und schlechte Seiten, aber das Land, das uns oft am meisten frustriert, ist das, in dem wir geboren wurden, aber erinnere dich daran, dass das deine eigene Wahl war, dort zu inkarnieren, und dies hatte einen Grund. Nachdem wir gereist sind und nach dem, was wir in anderen Teilen der Welt gesehen und gelernt haben, mögen wir vielleicht an unseren Geburtsort zurückkehren oder an einen anderen Seelenort, und wir mögen die Dinge dort ändern, wo es am notwendigsten ist—das kreieren, was wir sehen möchten, anstatt es anderswo zu suchen. Was neu und frisch ist, scheint immer besser zu sein, aber nur auf den ersten Blick, und du wirst feststellen, dass die Probleme, die wir haben, überall auf der Welt ähnlich sind und dass unsere Traumwelt nicht existiert, wenn wir sie nicht selbst kreieren—deswegen kamen wir hierher. Wir können zwischen verschiedenen Orten springen, an verschiedenen Orten leben, was das Leben viel aufregender macht, aber verliere nie dein Hier und Jetzt. Mutter Natur ist großartig überall und genau da, wo du jetzt stehst. Gieße sie, respektiere sie, schütze sie, liebe sie, tanze auf ihr, zusammen, *Soul Family*.

Erzgebirge, Deutschland, Dezember 2023

Riesiger, göttlicher, grenzenloser Raum

So wie ich durch das Fenster schaue, zähle ich neun Apfel-, drei Kirsch-, drei Pflaumen-, und drei Birnenbäume in voller Blüte in unserem Garten. Eine junge, orange Tigerkatze schleicht durch das hohe Gras auf der Jagd in der goldenen Abendsonne. Die friedliche Ruhe wird nur von ein paar zwitschernden Vögeln unterbrochen. Da draußen gibt es einen riesigen, göttlichen, grenzenlosen Raum für uns, um ihn mit süßem, süßem Leben zu füllen.

Erzgebirge, Deutschland, April 2023

Natur, du bist mein geliebtes Heim

Natur, Du bist mein geliebtes Heim
Mein Versteck, seit ich rennen kann
Weg von goldenen Schlössern und der
Gesellschaft in einer Box
Bin nicht hier, um deine Box bunt anzumalen
Ich gehe mit dem *Flow* des Flusses
Geblasen vom Wind
Dorthin, wo das Leben wächst
In meiner freien, bunten Welt

Erzgebirge, Deutschland, April 2023

April Regen

April Regen
Du hast meinen Schmerz weggewaschen
Ich saß in einem leeren Zug
Und die Natur war nicht mehr kahl
Löste meine Gedanken von alten Ketten
Das Reisen hat mich wieder befreit

Sachsen, Deutschland, April 2023

Gemeinschaftsgeist

Eine Geld-und selbstorientierte Gesellschaft tötet jeglichen Gemeinschaftsgeist. Je ärmer die Menschen, desto größer ist die Gemeinschaft meiner Erfahrung nach. Ich habe Gemeinschaft zwischen den Menschen in ihrer reinsten Form in Südamerika und Afrika erlebt, und es war auch der Ort, wo die Menschen am glücklichsten erschienen, obwohl sie am wenigsten besaßen. Ich weiß, dass es Gemeinschaftsgeist auch in Europa gibt, aber meiner Meinung nach ist er schwer zu finden. Dass das Teilen und etwas zusammen erschaffen glücklicher macht, als alles für dich allein zu haben, ist kein Geheimnis. Es gibt eine Vielzahl von neuen experimentellen Gemeinschaftsformen, die als Gegenreaktion zu einem komplett fehlenden Gemeinschaftsgedanken in unseren westlichen Kulturen, entstehen. Ich spreche über sogenannte *New Age* Kreise oder *Family* wie sie sich selbst nennen, die sich oft vom Rest abtrennen, da sie sich als anders oder oft sogar als besser betrachten, weswegen sie mich abstoßen, und auch weil sie oft eine weitere Form eines Extrems annehmen. Können wir uns bitte daran erinnern, was wahre Gemeinschaft ist? Dass es einfach nur bedeutet, dich um deinen Nachbarn zu kümmern und ein Bewusstsein über die Gesellschaft als ein Ganzes zu haben, die etwas zusammen erschafft und sich ergänzt, anstatt miteinander zu wetteifern oder um dem Anderen zu gefallen, mit diesem seltsamen Bedürfnis nicht aufzufallen, anstatt man selbst zu sein und dein höchstes Potenzial zu entfalten zum Wohle aller, und anstatt nur blind dem Geld hinterherzujagen? Ich glaube, dass wir hier sind, um ein Leben zu erschaffen, das auf Kreativität, Nachhaltigkeit, Freiheit und Unabhängigkeit vom alten Macht-und Kontrollsystem basiert zusammen mit unserem *Soul Tribe*—was nichts anderes bedeutet als mit unseren echten Freunden—mit Menschen, mit denen du auf der gleichen Wellenlänge bist, Verbindungen, die auf dem Herz basieren und nicht auf Ego mit einer Agenda, zusammen mit den Visionären, mit denjenigen, die sich daran erinnern, dass das Leben das größte Geschenk auf der Erde ist und dass wir hier sind, um es vollends zu leben—nicht um zu existieren, nicht um zu überleben, nicht um zu funktionieren, nicht um zu kaufen, sondern, um zu erblühen. Zusammen.

Erzgebirge, Deutschland, März 2023

Mit den Jahreszeiten gehen

Vielleicht lasse ich mich niemals nieder, weil ich mich nicht niederlassen sollte. Weil ich eine wahre Nomadin und ein Freigeist im Herzen bin, weil es nicht in meiner Natur liegt, mich einzuschließen in einer kleinen Betonschachtel und mich zwischen der Einkaufsstraße und der Arbeit zu bewegen—allein und unglücklich wie eine Sklavin einer Geldwelt, die Befehle und Pflichten erfüllt und Angst hat, aus der Reihe zu tanzen?! Vielleicht, weil meine Glaubenssätze so grenzenlos sind wie die Welt ist, deren Grenzen künstlich sind und niemals ein Hindernis für einen wahren Abenteurer sind. Vielleicht ist meine *Soul Family* überall auf der Welt verteilt, wo sie echte unabhängige, nachhaltige, glückliche Gemeinschaften aufbauen, um zwischen ihnen zu springen, auf und abspringen, sich mit den Jahreszeiten bewegen, wie sich die Tiere und Naturvölker bewegen—im Einklang mit dem Universum und dem natürlichen *Flow* des Lebens, weil das das neue, obwohl alte

Prinzip ist, das originale Muster des Lebens ist?! Vielleicht lasse ich mich nie nieder, weil die Welt erst erkundet werden muss, bevor ich mich niederlasse. Vielleicht lasse ich mich nie an einem einzigen Ort nieder, weil die Welt zu wunderschön ist, um nur an einem Ort zu leben, weil wir eine große, glückliche Familie sind, mit vielen verschiedenen Zügen und Farben, um uns gegenseitig zu ergänzen und um verschiedene Geschmäcke, Landschaften und Kulturen zu kosten?! Vielleicht sitze ich hier nicht allein, mit einem Haus, Mann und Kindern, weil ich alle Kinder dieser Welt liebe und nicht eines meins nennen muss. Vielleicht ist es, weil ich niemals wieder diese altmodische, langweilige Beziehung haben möchte, mich 365 Tage im Jahr um Haus und Garten kümmern, angebunden an einen einzigen Ort, was mich einschränken würde, und warum würde ich mir jemals wieder Gedanken um wie, wann, was, wo machen, anstatt einfach diese geniale Welle des Lebens zu reiten, meine Freunde?!

Erzgebirge, Deutschland, Mai 2023

Kosmische Kultur

Ich identifiziere mich nicht mit deutscher Kultur. Ich glaube nicht, dass ich mich mit irgendeiner Kultur identifiziere. Ich lebe wirklich meine eigene Kultur und nehme aus jeder Kultur, die ich erlebt habe, das Beste heraus. Natürlich bin ich auf großartige Weise von verschiedenen Kulturen inspiriert worden und habe einige meiner eigenen Züge in anderen Kulturen wiedererkannt, aber wie jedes vom Menschen erfundene Konzept, hat Kultur ihre Grenzen, aber ich bin grenzenlos und untypisch, weil ich deprogrammiert bin, das heißt frei. Ich liebe die deutsche Direktheit, die britische Exzentrik, die italienische Verspieltheit, die spanische Lockerheit und die afrikanische Coolness usw. jedoch unterscheiden sich Lebensweisen heutzutage nicht so stark in einer Welt, wo die Menschen hauptsächlich vom Geld angetrieben werden. Selbst an den abgelegensten Orten, mit genügend offenem Raum für einen kreativen Kopf, auf eintausend Ideen zu kommen, was man kreieren könnte, überarbeiten sich die Menschen trotzdem wie ein Roboter. Wie kannst Du nur so extrem programmiert sein, frage ich mich? Es ist diese Geld-und Stundenplan Mentalität die dir 4 bis 6 Wochen bezahlten Urlaub von deinem Leben erlaubt, bla bla. Ich verstehe, dass es unmöglich ist, mit einem erwachten Geist, so ein Leben zu führen. Niemand ist besser als jemand anderes. Aber wenn du bewusst bist, siehst du Geld als nichts weiter als ein Nebenprodukt. Wie konnten wir alle vergessen, dass es nur ein Mittel zum Zweck ist? Wie konntest du erlauben, dass es die Hauptrolle in deinem Leben einnehmen würde? Wie konntest du so abhängig vom Materialismus werden? Wie konntest du vergessen, was du als Kind wusstest? Was ist deine Leidenschaft? Was wirst du kreieren? Wir werden uns finden und das Neue zusammen bauen. Mit unserem *Soul Tribe* und wir werden eine neue Währung erfinden, einen neuen Luxus, eine Art von Magie.

Erzgebirge, Deutschland, Mai 2023

Heimat II

Ich gehe zurück nach Hause
Und niemand kann mich jemals
wieder verbannen
Von meinem Land
Wohin ich kam
Weil all das, was ich bin
In voller Sicht ist
Nie wieder
Versteckt
Und wenn es in eure eingezäunten
Köpfe nicht passt
Werde ich nicht mehr hassen
Weil ich darüber kreise
In meiner freien Welt
Wo ich eure Mauern der Angst
Mit Liebe
Durchbreche

Erzgebirge, Deutschland, Mai 2023

Freier Garten

Ich habe so viele Länder bereist und traf und lebte mit so vielen verschiedenen Nationalitäten zusammen, dass, anstatt so wie irgendeine von denen zu werden, anstatt eine zu lieben und eine andere zu hassen, du einfach immer mehr du selbst wirst. Du stellst fest, dass viel von dem, was du in anderen Leuten siehst, kulturelle Programmierung ist, nicht so wie die Menschen geboren wurden—frei—und je größer das Bild wird, dass du bekommst, umso weißer und ruhiger wirst du. Du wirst zu einem Beobachter. Einige Kulturen inspirieren dich und andere stoßen dich eher ab—je nachdem, was zu deinem Charakter passt, und du rennst weg von dem, was nicht zu dir passt, bis du begreifst, dass das Einzige vor dem du wegrennen kannst, du selbst bist. Du hast gelernt, dass du nur das hassen kannst, was ein Teil von dir ist, bis es nichts mehr zu hassen gibt. Die Art und Weise, wie Glaubenssysteme, soziale und politische Systeme funktionieren und Menschen formen, kann dich nur frustrieren, wenn du daran Teil nimmst, aber die Welt ist kein Land, keine Regierung oder Nation, die dich besitzen darf. Dies sind künstliche Konzepte auf der Grundlage von Trennung, Klassifizierung und aus den alten Macht-und Kontrollenergien geboren, die dich nicht mehr kontrollieren oder entmachten können, wenn du verstehst, dass die Welt ein freier Garten voller Fülle ist, in dem du blühen und tanzen kannst, und dass du immer deine eigene Realität selbst kreierst durch deine eigenen Glaubenssätze und dass du freien Willen hast zu wählen, woran du Teil nimmst und woran nicht. Es gibt kein perfektes Land, kein perfektes System oder keine perfekte Nation, sondern die Erde ist überall wunderschön und göttlich, der Rest ist unsere ganz eigene Kreation. Ich habe mich so oft gefragt, warum ich mich dazu entschied, in einem Land zu inkarnieren, das mir am wenigsten frei erschien, verglichen mit all den anderen Orten, die ich gesehen habe, und mit den Deutschen, die so beschränkt und gefangen in ihren perfekt organisierten Köpfen erscheinen, was konsequenterweise zu einem Fehlen von Herz, Leidenschaft und Freude führt, und ich habe verstanden, dass es eine meiner größten Herausforderungen war, und meine Herzensmission dieses Land zu wählen. Zuhause war für mich nie ein Land, eine Nation, oder das kulturelle Konzept eines Ortes, sondern nichts anderes als das freie Land—die Energie der Erde, die Felder und Wälder, die Wesen der Natur und das Mythische, die Liebe, Tradition und Geborgenheit—der Ort, den ich mein Zuhause nenne und der keine Grenzen kennt von Freiheit und Liebe. Und ich verstehe, dass ich hier auch alles andere was mir meine Freiheit versuchte zu nehmen, liebe, weil ich sie mir so gänzlich zurückholte, und weil es mein Traum war, der Welt zu zeigen, wie man frei ist, als Wegbereiterin, als Visionärin, als Pionierin. Aus Liebe.

Erzgebirge, Deutschland, Juni 2023

Mutter Erde

Als Kind haben unsere Eltern und Großeltern meine Schwester und mich oft zum Pilze sammeln in den großen, wunderschönen Erzgebirgswald mitgenommen, in dem wir für Stunden tief eintauchten, ohne viel zu sprechen, wo wir zu einem Teil unserer Umwelt wurden, und ich erinnere mich daran, wie ich eine tiefe Ehrfurcht vor dem großen, mythischen Wald spürte, und ich mache immer noch das Gleiche und es macht mich wirklich glücklich. Wenn man in der ehemaligen DDR, wie ich aufwuchs, war Selbstversorgung ganz normal. Fast jeder bebaute einen Garten und hatte Tiere, mit denen er zusammenlebte. Jetzt sind die ganze Permakultur und *Off-Grid*-Bewegung fast schon ein Trend als Antwort auf ein konsumorientiertes Stadtleben, abgetrennt von der Natur, geworden, und mir gefällt weder das eine, noch das andere Extrem. Für mich ist es das Normalste der Welt, in der Natur zu leben, auch wahrscheinlich, weil ich auf dem Land aufwuchs, wo es normal ist, essbare Pflanzen, Beeren und Pilze zu kennen, weswegen ich Parks und Spielplätze immer lächerlich fand. Anstatt wie ein Tourist die Natur zu besuchen, bin ich immer zurückgekommen, um mitten in der Natur zu leben, und ich habe sie immer beobachtet und von ihr gelernt. Sie ist meine größte Inspiration, meine größte Heilerin und Lehrerin. Die Menschheit hat vergessen, dass sie der Boden ist, auf dem du stehst, die Luft, die du atmest, das Haus, in dem du lebst, die Ruhe und Balance, die du in dir findest. Respektiere deine Mutter. Mutter Erde.

Erzgebirge, Deutschland, Juli 2023

Mein Sommer

Mein Sommer
Wie wiegst Du schwer
Und ich mag nicht sprechen mehr
Bäume flüstern
Blätter winken
Gräser tanzen
Im Abendlicht
Wieso siehst Du sie nicht?
Mein Sommer, ich lieb' Dich so sehr.

Erzgebirge, Deutschland, Juli 2023

Mutig und frei

Bin wirklich stolz auf mich, dass ich fast alle meine Reisen allein gemacht habe. Begann in einem frühen Alter ins Ausland zu reisen, schlief in meinem Auto unter den Sternen und in eintausend verschiedenen Betten, wartete nie auf *Prince Charming*, mich umherzutragen, lehnte fast alle Einladungen zu Luxusurlauben ab, von Typen mit einer gewissen Absicht, und arbeitete in einhundert verschiedenen Jobs, um meine Reisen zu finanzieren. Habe viele besondere Menschen auf der ganzen Welt getroffen und habe be*chissene Dinge erlebt, das wahre Leben in seinen Extremen, während ich meine eigenen Ängste und Grenzen überwand, wodurch ich um ganze Leben wuchs, mit diesem Adrenalin, das durch deinen Körper rast auf diesem einzigen zu habenden Taxi auf dem Hintersitz eines Motorrades durch die Favelas von Rio mit diesem einheimischen Typ, mit diesen in den Bann ziehenden, grünen Augen, um Jesus zu sehen. Ich könnte eine Million Storys erzählen und ich bin noch nicht ganz fertig.

Erzgebirge, Deutschland, Juli 2023

IV. Ost Wärts

Hungrig nach Inspiration

Ich bin froh, dass ich einen neuen Sprung wagte, raus aus meinem kleinen, sicheren Hafen, meinem versteckten üppigen Naturparadies zu Hause auf dem Land in Ostdeutschland bei meiner Familie und Freunden, die ich über alles liebe, wo jedoch jeder den westlichen *Lifestyle* auf der Überholspur lebt—leben um zu arbeiten, völlig geblendet von der materiellen Welt und komplett abgetrennt vom Geist und ich vermisse furchtbar echte Inspiration von Leuten, die eine spirituelle Praxis und eine *Work-Life Balance*—Glück—in ihr Leben integriert haben—die die Geheimnisse des Kosmos studieren, anstatt der heutigen Shopping-Schnäppchen und Instagram *posts* und ich kann es nicht erwarten, sie in Zentralasien zu finden. Ich fühle einen großen, göttlichen, offenen Raum und lächelnde Menschen, die mich rufen, und ich werde sie mit dem Kompass meines Herzens finden.

Mascat, Oman, August 2023

Freies Tibet

In einer besonderen Begegnung, die ich mit zwei Tibetern in Nepal's belebtem Hauptplatz auf den Stufen einer der vielen atemberaubenden Tempeln hatte, der eine verrückte Verschmelzung von Kathmandu's hektischem, täglichen Leben mit seinem faszinierendem spirituellem Leben ist, glaube ich mehr gelernt zu haben, als manche Menschen es in ihren Ashrams und spirituellen Retreats in mehreren Wochen tun—durch das schönste Lächeln, der Liebe und Leichtherzigkeit, die das kleine Tibetische Mädchen ausstrahlte, zusammen mit ihrem Vater, der mir ein handgemachtes Buch auf Tibetisch gab, welches ich nicht lesen kann, mit vielen Kamasutra Zeichnungen und durch das bezaubernde Flötenspiel der Kinder, mit den höchsten, freudigsten Tönen, die ich jemals hörte, und denen ich in einen der Tempel folgte, wodurch ich mehr die Seele der Tibetischen Kultur spürte, als ich es vielleicht auf einer organisierten, überwachten teuren, touristischen Gruppentour hätte—die einzige Möglichkeit nach Tibet zu kommen—und wogegen ich mich entschied, weil das Geld dafür an die chinesische Regierung gehen würde, welche die tibetische Kultur zerstört und Tausende ins Exil zwang. Egal wie hart das Leben ist—Nepal ist eines der ärmsten Länder der Welt—und wie unfair und korrupt diejenigen sind, die die Welt regieren—renne frei und glücklich wie das kleine tibetische Mädchen.

Kathmandu, Nepal, August 2023

Heiligkeit können sie nicht erobern

Ich habe Glück, dass Licht und fließendes Wasser hier in meinem 3-Dollar Zimmer in Pokhara nicht ausfallen, wo ich am Fuß der 8000 Meter hohen Annapurna Gebirgskette bin, wie in Kathmandu, von wo ich auf dem schlimmsten 8-stündigen Bustrip meines Lebens entlang der Hauptverkehrsader des Landes kam und entschied später, einen Flug zurück in die Hauptstadt zu nehmen, weil ich nicht hunderte Meter tief, von der unbefestigten Straße in das Flussbett fallen möchte, so wie es hier öfter passiert. Warum ist Nepal eines der ärmsten Länder der Welt trotz des Millionen Dollar Business mit der Besteigung des Mount Everest, das zwischen 40000 und 100000 Dollar kostet, mit hunderten Bergsteigern pro Woche?! In Tempeln herumzusitzen und Buddha zu imitieren reicht nicht, wenn wir die korrupten, führenden Politiker dieser Welt stoppen wollen. Du musst aufstehen und dir deine Macht zurückholen. Nicht indem du den heiligen

Himalaya eroberst, sondern indem du in deiner heiligen Kraft von innen stehst und handelst. Ich bin am Fuß der heiligen Machhapuchre, der einer der wenigen Gipfel ist, die nicht bestiegen werden dürfen. Heiligkeit können sie nicht erobern.

Pokhara, Nepal, September 2023

Erwache zu deiner wahren Kraft

Für mich ist Urlaub eine Pause vom Hamsterrad, eine Pause von deinem Leben, für das sie dich hart bezahlen lassen, aber im Leben geht es um mehr, als im Dienst und außer Dienst zu sein. Im Leben geht es um Selbstverwirklichung, und eine echte Reise ist ein spiritueller Weg der Selbst-und Entdeckung der Welt, für dein Wachstum und deine Inspiration auf dem Weg der Einheit, während du mehr lernst, als sie dir jemals beibringen können. Selbstverwirklichung ist deine Bestimmung zu leben, was auch immer deine Begabung, Talente und Leidenschaften sein mögen, und Geld ist ein Nebenprodukt davon, nichts weiter als ein Mittel zum Zweck, anstatt der primäre Fokus in einer *Work-Life Balance*—vergiss nicht zu lächeln, meditieren, singen, beten, laufen, essen, atmen, zu lieben in Einheit mit Mutter Erde und allen Formen des Lebens, anstatt von Selbstzerstörung. Die Dame, bei der ich in den nepalesischen Bergen wohne, holt den Mais, den Tee und die Tomaten aus ihrem Garten heraus, um sie in der Sonne zu trocknen. Ich denke über das westliche Trauma nach, während ich die Wunder der Welt anblicke—die Gipfel des Himalaya von meinem Zimmer aus, das mich 5 Dollar am Tag kostet, während andere denken, sie könnten sich niemals einen Nepal-Urlaub leisten, für den sie tausende Dollar wollen auf einem organisierten Trip. Folge dem Programm oder erwache zu deiner wahren Kraft.

Annapurna, Himalaya, Nepal, September 2023

Himalaya

Himalaya
Du stehst in deiner heiligen Kraft tief verwurzelt
in der Mutter mit deiner Krone im Himmel
Du kämpfst nicht um dein Recht
Stehst in deiner heiligen Gegenwart
Erinnerst mich daran, wer ich bin
Om Namah Shivaya
Himalaya

Annapurna, Himalaya, Nepal, September 2023

Mein Nomadenherz schlägt schneller

Mein Nomadenherz schlägt schneller, seit ich meinen Fuß auf mongolische Erde setzte. Schon immer hat mein Herz sich danach gesehnt, unter dem großen, weiten Himmel des endlosen Landes im Rhythmus mit den Elementen, den Jahreszeiten, mit den Tieren und im natürlichen Fluss des Lebens zu leben—wirklich eine alte Liebe. Mein ganzes Leben lang war ich am glücklichsten draußen—jenseits kleiner Betonschachteln, Mauern und Rahmen. Nirgendwo fühlst du dich freier, als wenn du in einer traditionellen Jurte aufwachst, mit dutzenden Adlern, die über dir kreisen, und mit der frischesten Luft, die du je geatmet hast, und auf dem Rücken eines wilden, mongolischen Pferdes über das endlose, heitere, wunderschöne Grasland fliegend. Für mich ist das einer der inspirierendsten Orte, die ich je bereiste, auch, weil es das am wenigsten verwestlichteste und globalisierteste Land ist, das ich je erlebte. Das mongolische Volk hat ihre ganz eigene, stolze, starke, individuelle und unabhängige Identität bewahrt und sie sind die süßesten und coolsten Leute, die ich jemals traf—sie sind unglaublich gastfreundlich, nett, offen und schlau, was an ihrer Lebensweise liegt und daran, dass sie ihren eigenen kritischen Verstand benutzen, anstatt von den Medien und sozialen Normen und Zwängen programmiert zu sein. Sie sehen überhaupt nicht arm aus, sondern eher wohlhabend, und sie ziehen sich gut und irgendwie cool an—du siehst sie in diesen langen, bunten Seidenmänteln mit einem Gürtel und einem Hut und Sonnenbrille auf ihren *vintage* Motorrädern. Ich bin in der ehemaligen Hauptstadt des riesigen, weiten, alten, mongolischen Reiches was ich erst herausfand, als ich das einzigartige Buddhistische Erdene Zuu Kloster aus dem 16. Jahrhundert besuchte, und ich wohne in einer Jurte, die ich von einer netten, einheimischen Familie miete, deren Kinder mir super reif, unabhängig und schlau vorkommen und die auf den ganzen Ort allein aufpassen, während ihr Vater einfach für ein paar

Tage raus in die Wildnis geht—etwas, was ganz normal ist in der Mongolei. Das Land hat nur drei Millionen Einwohner, von denen ein Drittel ein Nomadenleben führt, und die Städte haben nur eine Handvoll von Läden, wo sie lokale Produkte verkaufen und das, was gebraucht wird, anstatt von Massenkonsum und Verschwendung. Das Nomadenleben ist in Wahrheit die nachhaltigste, verantwortungsvollste, und bewussteste Lebensweise, die es gibt, im Gegensatz zu einer archaisch, kolonialen, westlichen Einstellung überlegen zu sein, und sie ist die Zukunft. Wenig besitzen und alles haben. Freiheit.

Kharkhorin, Mongolei, September 2023

Weg der Mitte

Bin wirklich stolz auf mich, dass ich einen Weg fand, um die Welt mit wenig Geld zu bereisen, was mich vor den Haupttouristenfallen bewahrte, wo ein Bild eines Landes verkauft wird, das wenig mit der Realität zu tun hat. Ich weiß, dass Leute in den Urlaub fahren, um eine Pause von ihrem normalen Leben zu machen, wo Cocktails und Swimmingpool wahrscheinlich funktionieren, aber ich lebe ein Leben, von dem ich keine Pause brauche, und ich reise für das Abenteuer, für Inspiration und um meine Ansichten zu erweitern. Ich suche immer nach der lokalen Erfahrung, und so behandeln sie mich wie eine von ihnen, was wirklich mein Herz berührt, wenn ich merke, dass ich Fremden wichtig bin und mit offenen Armen empfangen werde, was ich so oft auf der ganzen Welt erlebte, besonders an Orten, wo echte Gemeinschaft noch mehr zählt als Geld. Um wirklich fremde Orte kennenzulernen, musst du dich mit den Einheimischen vermischen, und das passiert hier in der Mongolei von ganz allein, da die Leute so herzlich und offen sind, was von ihren reisenden Nomadenstämmen und Lebensstil herrührt—nichts öffnet dein Herz und deinen Verstand mehr. Ich wurde von den süßesten Kindern umarmt, in Häuser eingeladen, habe Essen geteilt, und tauschte so viel Lächeln aus und kommunizierte mit Zeichensprache und vor allem mit der Sprache des Herzens, die jeder versteht. Ich habe noch nie so offene, freundliche, freie und glückliche Kinder gesehen. Ich glaube, dass das alle Kinder von Natur aus sind, aber die Erziehung macht aus vielen ängstliche, eingeschüchterte oder sogar böse Kinder. Hier siehst du sie alle zusammen draußen spielen, und sie lächeln dich automatisch an, wenn sie dich sehen, wohingegen sie wegschauen würden dort, woher ich komme. Hier kamen sie zu mir gerannt, mit ihren großen, neugierigen Herzen. Sie haben mich mit Pinienkernen gefüttert, Bilder mit meiner Nikon gemacht, mich umarmt und nicht aufgehört, mit mir zu reden, obwohl ich nichts verstand außer: „Wo sind deine Eltern?" In der Natur aufzuwachsen, in Gemeinschaft und mit Tieren, hat riesige positive Effekte auf Kinder. Die unglaublich unbesorgten, leichtherzigen, freudigen und freien Kinder haben mich tief berührt und mich daran erinnert, auch so zu sein, rauszugehen und zu spielen und Spaß zu haben und das Leben nicht so ernst zu nehmen. Ich habe auch eine gesunde, leichte, spirituelle Praxis in der Mongolei bemerkt—nicht so extreme religiöse Programmierung wie ich es in anderen Länder beobachtet habe, sondern auf eine natürliche Art—ich nenne es leichten oder gesunden Buddhismus und stelle fest, dass wir die gleichen Glaubenssätze haben, ohne dass ich ihn je in Büchern studiert hätte, sondern seine großen, universellen Wahrheiten selbst entdeckte, indem ich den Weg des Herzens ging und durch die Entdeckung meines Selbst und der Welt. In Asien Leute zu sehen, die ihre Mantras auf dem Bürgersteig singen und tanzen, zu ihren Göttern beim Kochen sprechen oder meditierend auf den Straßen und Plätzen sitzend, ist die normalste Sache der Welt, wohingegen du für verrückt gehalten würdest, wenn du das Gleiche im Westen tun würdest. Es ist wirklich an der Zeit für jeden, den großen Geist zu verstehen und die kosmischen Gesetze, wenn du weniger Geld für Alkohol, Pillen und Psychologen ausgeben willst. Die Mongolei inspiriert mich, insbesondere weil ich bemerke, wie die Leute hier noch ihren eigenen kritischen Verstand anwenden, im Gegensatz zu so viel Programmierung in der westlichen Welt, wo die Leute einfach blindlings der Matrix folgen, wohingegen hier sich das Leben natürlich anfühlt, voller Sinn und Seele. Echt.

Kharkhorin, Mongolei, September 2023

Ritt in die Freiheit

Gestern heuerte ich einen Einheimischen auf einem Motorrad an, um mich hinaus zu den Bergen zu fahren, indem ich einfach in die Richtung am Horizont zeigte, die faszinierend aussah, und es war keine gute Idee, dahin zu laufen, da alles, was nah in der Mongolei aussieht, sehr weit entfernt ist. Wir kommunizierten in Zeichensprache und ich gab ihm 10 Dollar, da das die Art und Weise ist, die ich lernte, wie man reist aus dem ursprünglichen Grund, dass ich nie viel Geld hatte, was mich davor bewahrte in die Haupttouristenfallen zu stürzen und wo ich lernte mutig zu sein, gesunden Menschenverstand anzuwenden, meine Umwelt zu beobachten und auf meine Intuition zu hören, was besser ist als jeder bezahlte Touristenführer der Welt und die beste Garantie für Abenteuer und um ein Land wirklich kennenzulernen, so wie es ist, anstatt eines falschen verkauften Bildes für Touristen und es gab mir die Möglichkeit zu lernen und wachsen, über mich selbst hinaus auf die größte

Art und Weise, anstatt Sehenswürdigkeiten auf einer Liste abzuhaken, die andere für wichtig halten! Mein Fahrer brachte mich zum schönsten, versteckten Ort mit einer unglaublich klaren Energie, wo Mönche einige kleine, buddhistische Tempel errichteten, da sie den Berg als heilig erkannten. Auf meinem Ritt durch das freie, weite Grasland fuhr ich an einigen Nomadenjurten und Kamelen und vielen Schafen und Ziegen vorbei, mit meinem freundlichen Fahrer, der ein paar Lieder summte, während ich mir dachte, ich könnte hier leben, *lol*. Derjenige, der die Angst vor dem Unbekannten überwindet, wird mit der größten Freiheit, Spaß und Magie beschenkt.

Kharkhorin, Mongolei, September, 2023

Land der Freiheit

Mongolei
Mein Herz sehnte sich nach dem Land
der Freiheit
Das ich wiedererkannte
Durch die brennende Flamme in mir
Die entzündet wurde wie nie zuvor
Als ich die endlose Steppe und das
Grasland wiedersah
Schimmernd im goldenen Licht
Wo nur der Horizont meinen Namen ruft
Wo wir unter einer Million Sterne am
Feuer sitzen
Unsere Herzen teilen
Die ewige Liebe
Für das Land der Freiheit
Die für immer brennt

Kharkhorin, Mongolei, September 2023

Einst war ich Schamane

Ich weiß, dass
In einem anderen Leben
Ich Schamane war
Irgendwo zwischen der magischen,
mongolischen Steppe und den tiefen
Wäldern Sibiriens
Ich konnte mit den Adlern fliegen, mit den
Pferden rennen, mit den Geistern tanzen
Ich konnte alles tun
Jetzt zerschneide ich alle Ketten, die die
Menschheit gefangen halten
Die alten Türme der Macht und Kontrolle fallen
Die Neue Erde blüht und alle ihre Kinder rennen
wieder frei

Kharkhorin, Mongolei, September 2023

Nomade aus Natur

Ich dachte, ich würde nächstes Jahr weniger reisen, aber wie kann man jemals aufhören, wenn man einmal Freiheit geschmeckt hat? Was mich am meisten inspiriert in der Welt sind echte, freundliche positive, offene Menschen und ich habe so viele warmherzige Leute auf meinen Reisen um die Welt getroffen, und sehr oft hier in der Mongolei, wo sie mich einfach zu einem Teil von ihnen gemacht haben, mich eingeladen haben, um mit ihnen zusammen zu sitzen und zu essen, als sie mich am Straßenrand auf einen Bus wartend sahen, mitten im Nirgendwo, mich persönlich ans andere Ende der Hauptstadt Ulan Bator brachten, als ich nach der Richtung fragte und all die anderen süßen Begegnungen, die ich niemals vergessen werde—sie werden alles mit dir teilen wo Kapitalismus und Egoismus die Herzen noch nicht verdorben haben. Obwohl ich anders als sie aussehe, urteilen sie dich hier nicht nach dem, wie du aussiehst, sondern erkennen dich als Reisender, den sie mit offenen Armen empfangen, und es gibt keine andere Absicht hinter ihren Handlungen als die von Mitgefühl und Liebe—das ganze Gegenteil von der Kultur, in die ich geboren wurde und aus wessen Grund ich dort niemals Vollzeit leben möchte—einfach gehen und bleiben wie ein Nomade in seiner Jurte auf dem freien Land, wann und wohin auch immer er geleitet wird von der Natur, seiner Intuition und Weisheit.

Kharkhorin, Mongolei, September 2023

Seele Sibiriens

Heilige Brise
Trägt goldene Blätter fröhlicher Birkenbäume
Die den Teppich des weichen Sandes bestreuen
An dein Ufer gewaschen
Aus deinen kristallklaren Wassern
Aus den Tiefen deiner Seele
Wo ich allein tanze
Mit den Geistern
In lichtdurchfluteten Wäldern aus
Lärche und Pinie
Heiliger Baikal
Hier und überall
Glorreiche Schöpfung
Feiern

Maksimikha, Baikalsee, Sibirien, Russland, 2023

Nach Goryachinsk getrampt

Bin nach Goryachinsk getrampt. Baikalsee, Ostseite, wo die Transsibirische Eisenbahn keine ausländischen Touristen ausspuckt, die nicht mehr kommen, sondern wo ich ganz allein bin, zusammen mit den paar Einheimischen. Echter wird es nicht. Den Schmuck lasse ich besser im Zimmer. Die Kamera auch. Du kannst nie wissen. Du lernst das, wenn du die Welt allein bereist—nimm nicht dieses Risiko. Andere nimmst Du. Wie nach Russland zu fahren, wenn der Ruf stärker ist als die Angst, die sie zu verbreiten versuchen. Allein in Sibirien zu reisen ist sicherer als irgendeine Großstadt in meinem Heimatland Deutschland, und du verlierst die Angst, wenn du allein um die Welt reist—immer mehr vertraust du deiner eigenen Intuition und wirst stark auf deinem Weg und sanft im Herzen. Wo auch immer du hingehst, sind die Leute nett zu dir, weil du es bist, und du fühlst dich unendlich frei. Jeder Tag bringt eine neue Entdeckung über dich selbst und die Welt.

Der Baikalsee, der tiefste, älteste und klarste See der Welt, ist ein Wunder—Du musst ihn in seiner Weisheit und Kraft erleben—umgeben von dichtem, endlosen Taigawald und Sibirien ist sibirisch. Magisch und einsam. Es gibt mehr Wodka als frisches Essen, sie essen Buchweizen anstatt Reis, die Häuser sind aus Holz, die Tischdecken gehäkelt und die Leute denken, ich bin Russin, bis ich zu sprechen beginne. Wenn es nicht gemütlich ist, dann ist es trostlos. Ein Zwischenspiel wie das Leben selbst. Viele Leute ziehen in die Stadt bis sie verstehen werden, dass das Leben dort sogar noch einsamer als in Sibirien ist, wenn ihr euch nicht die Hände reicht—falle nicht in die kapitalistische Falle—Lenins Idee von sozialer Gerechtigkeit war gut aber er bedachte nicht, dass sie nicht von oben diktiert werden kann, sondern von unten aufsteigt—vom tiefen Verständnis in dir, dass wir alle gleich sind und dass die wahre Kraft in deinem eigenen Herzen und Händen liegt und wenn du die Schönheit, anstatt der Einsamkeit deines sibirischen Dorfes siehst—deine Freiheit ist deine Unabhängigkeit. Jeder hier weiß, dass der Krieg ein *Business* der Regierenden der Welt ist, aber sie haben keine Macht, wenn du ihnen keine Macht gibst.

Turka, Baikalsee, Sibirien, Russland, Oktober 2023

Freiheit

Jeder kann an einer Hotelbar sitzen und einen Cocktail bestellen, aber nicht jeder kann Abgeschiedenheit ertragen. Du allein an einem Ort, wo niemand hingehen will, weil niemand ihn jemals in einem Touristenführer erwähnt hat. Die Leute sind wie Schafe. Sie folgen der Herde blindlings, aber ich bin wie ein einsamer Wolf, der seinen Instinkten folgt, um die Welt zu entdecken und seine Herde weise aussucht. Der Stadtmensch landet in einem Bus in der Schönheit der Wildnis und seine erste Bemerkung wird sein: hier gibt es nichts. Der Wolf versteht, dass das Nichts alles ist. Er hört die Elemente sprechen, den Wind, die Wellen, die Bäume, die anderen Tiere, und er sitzt ruhig und hört dem Nichts zu, dass seine Magie demjenigen enthüllt, der zuhört jenseits von Zeit. Stille spricht. Er braucht keinen Zaun um sich herum, um sich sicher zu fühlen, sondern er liebt es, durch die Weite zu ziehen. Er vertraut darauf, dass er einen Freund trifft, wie ihn.

Turka, Baikalsee, Sibirien, Russland, Oktober 2023

Schamanisches Ritual

In Asien ist es ganz normal, spirituelle Praxis im täglichen Leben zu beobachten. Du siehst die Leute draußen ihre Mantras singen, überall in der Öffentlichkeit in die Meditation gehend, neben der Schnellstraße, mit einer Schüssel Milch im tiefen Gebet versunken stehend, oder du wirst zu einem Teil eines schamanischen Rituals gemacht, wie es mir heute passierte. Eine Gruppe von Freunden des heimischen Buryat Stammes, die eine sehr starke schamanische Tradition haben, winkte mich herüber, als ich auf einem Spaziergang durch den Wald an der Küste des Baikalsees entlang ging und als sie mich auf einem Felsen sitzend sahen, ihrem Trommeln zuhörend. Sie gaben mir *Chai und* Häppchen zum Essen, die sie dabei hatten. Der Baikalsee und die Geister wurden durch Singen verehrt und mit Wodka, großen Torten, Zigaretten, Kleidern, Tee und mehr beschenkt. Die Schamanin—Schamanin von Geburt und ein ganz normales Mädchen und kein selbsternannter, narzisstischer, westlicher, teurer

Guru, die zu den Naturgeistern sprach—ging in Trance und channelte den Geist und segnete alle aus der Gruppe. Auf ganz natürliche Weise wurde ich zu einem Teil der Zeremonie gemacht—ganz egal mein Hintergrund, meine Herkunft oder mein Glauben—einfach weil ich gerade dort war, vom Geist geführt, wie immer natürlich. Es war ein Traum, der in Erfüllung ging. Ich bin sehr stark zu dieser Kultur hingezogen, weil es den Geist mit der Natur verbindet, und mit Kreativität, Musik und Tanz. Soo viel schöner als in einer Kirche zu sitzen und zu einem Sünder gemacht zu werden. Es ist wunderschön und berührend zu sehen, wie Menschen ihre Religion mit dir teilen und zum Geist und ihren Göttern im täglichen Leben sprechen. Wenn ich irgendetwas Ähnliches in der Öffentlichkeit in Deutschland tun würde, würde man mich für verrückt erklären in einer Kultur, die sich komplett vom Geist abgetrennt hat und ihre wahre Natur vergessen hat, als Teil des großen Ganzen. Tanz, Gebet, Natur, Ausdruck, Gemeinschaft. Menschliche kosmische Natur.

Turka, Baikalsee, Sibirien, Russland, Oktober 2023

Spirituelle Meisterklasse

Diese Asienreise ist nicht nur eines meiner größten Abenteuer, auf dem ich in die unterschiedlichsten Kulturen eintauche, die mich inspirieren und meinen Horizont auf die größte Art und Weise erleuchten, es ist eine spirituelle Meisterklasse. Auf der einen Seite ist da Tokyo, wo ich mich wie in einem apokalyptischen Film fühlte—die Matrix mit ihren robotermäßigen Menschen, die sich in perfekter Ordnung zwischen einem endlosen Meer von Wolkenkratzern bewegen, und dann ist da dieses andere Japan—eine andere Realität, die echt schmeckt, mit ihren üppigen Bergen und Feng Shui, da ist der Daoismus und die Qi Energie, in die ich hineinfühle. Es gibt so viele verschiedene Lehren in dieser Welt und ich beobachte, wie viele Studenten zu einem hingebungsvollen Schüler werden—ein Sklave einer Doktrin—ob es die buddhistischen Mönche oder die *New Age Hippies* sind. In meinen Augen nimmt spirituelle Praxis häufig zu extreme Formen an. Meiner Meinung nach, ist es nichts, dass für sich gelebt werden muss. Für mich geht es wirklich nicht um das eine oder andere Glaubenssystem, dem man sein völliges Recht gibt. Dies sind die Grenzen der Glaubenssysteme, oft mit einem narzisstischen Bedürfnis verbunden, im Recht zu sein, und wenn irgendeine Lehre dich als überzeugten Anhänger sehen will, es ist nicht mehr weise, sondern entmachtend, kontrollierend. Anstatt ein Anhänger der einen oder anderen Strömung zu werden, habe ich die Geheimnisse des Lebens durch Innenschau und Beobachtung des Außens studiert, meines Selbst und auf meinen Reisen um die Welt, und ich empfing sehr viel Wissen und Weisheit, wovon ich das meiste energetisch aufnahm und durch Beobachtung, anstatt ein Anhänger von jemandem zu sein, der Recht haben muss, und ich bin begeistert von dem, was ich empfange. Weder werde ich mich zum Hinduismus, noch zum Buddhismus oder Daoismus bekehren, so wie ich es nicht zum Protestantismus tat oder ein *New Age Hippie* wurde, sondern viele verschiedene Aspekte integrierte, weil ich weder das eine, noch das andere bin, sondern all das, was mich immens inspirierte und begeisterte, weil es Teile meiner eigenen kosmischen Seele sind. Orte können Energie haben, die Information aus dem Licht oder von Landschaften tragen, und dann gibt es Orte der Matrix ohne Energie wie Großstädte, wo sich die Menschen wie Roboter in einem Schema bewegen, und was sich wie ein apokalyptischer Film anfühlt, und dann gibt es da diesen Traum. Diese andere Realität. Den Himmel auf Erden. Ich kann die Weisheit und das Wissen von Bäumen channeln, von der Energie eines Ortes, von Musik oder Tempeln oder Steinen, die alle eine bestimmte Energie haben, die du auflesen kannst, anstatt ein Student tausender Bücher, die andere schrieben zu werden. Ich las Tausende von Seiten während meines Studiums an der Universität und jetzt schreibe ich meine eigenen Bücher, die nicht über mich sind, sondern für dich geschrieben, um dich an dich selbst zu erinnern.

Oshino Hakkai, Japan, Oktober 2023

Fujiyama

Silberne Bambusblütenfelder leuchten in der
Ferne an deinem Fuß
Deine weiße Schneekuppe versteckst du heute
in den Wolken
Ich konnte den Weg nicht finden
Da radelte ich hinaus und lag auf einer Wiese an
einem Bach
Da gab es eine Brücke
Mit Bambusblüten auf der anderen Seite
Ich lief hinüber
Und du warst ganz nah bei mir
Fujiyama
Du bliest die Wolken weg

Oshino Hakkai, Japan, Oktober 2023

Apokalyptische Show

Tokyo
Du verschließt deine Eintrittsgeldparks in der
Nacht und fährst deine Menschen an Sonntagen
in Bussen hinaus, um eingezäunte Natur zu
besuchen, Münzen in Schreine zu werfen und
nach Souvenirs zu jagen.
Es ist trendy, wie eine Kopie eines falschen
Comic-Königs oder Königin herumzulaufen.
Deine Bäume sprechen lauter, die Drachen
lachen und deine Bergketten wachsen über
deine Wolkenkratzer hinaus.
Deine Zukunft fühlt sich apokalyptisch an, Baby!

Tokyo, Japan, Oktober 2023

Tam Coc Heldin

Iss wie ein *Local*, was bedeutet vietnamesische Nudelsuppe zum Frühstück, weil du riesig enttäuscht sein wirst von irgendeiner Kopie westlichen Essens, das nur für die internationalen Touristen in diesem Teil der Welt gemacht wird—nein, ich bin keiner von denen! Die meisten von ihnen wirst du in den gleichen Ho(s)tels, Restaurants und Aktivitätenspots gruppiert antreffen, Online-Bewertungen und Empfehlungen folgend, auf ihr Telefon stierend, während sie die Straße überqueren—ich frage mich, wie viele von der Flut von Motorrädern überfahren werden—kein Schritt ohne Google Maps—niemals ohne das Telefon—aber du hast vergessen, wie man einen Telefonanruf macht. Der Held ist nicht der Instagrammer vom Banana Tree Swimmingpool Hotel, sondern die vietnamesische Lady, die zusammen mit den anderen in ihrem Boot jeden Tag hunderte Touristen zu einem einst bezauberndem Ort in der Natur rudert, welcher ausgesaugt wurde—eine

Art von nicht integrativem — nicht nachhaltigem, profitzentriertem Tourismus — ich nenne ihn Neokolonialismus — den ich nicht unterstütze. Nein, das ist nicht Vietnam! Sein alter Charme existiert noch — ich fand ihn in dem Lächeln der Gesichter und in den Ecken, wohin niemand schaut, und während du dem Bus an deine nächste Station oder zum nächsten buddhistischen Tempel nachjagst, liege ich hier im Sonnenschein, umgeben von den wunderschönen Tam Coc Felsen, den fallenden Blättern zuschauend, den Blumen und Schmetterlingen, während ich die buddhistische Art, die in jedem Moment ist, lebe. Sei kein Anhänger, sei ein Führer. Ein Führer des Herzens.

Tam Coc, Vietnam, Oktober 2023

Sie hält den Schlüssel

Mein wunderschönes, sanftes, unschuldiges Vietnam. Ich habe deine Seele erblickt und mich in dich am letzten Tag verliebt, nachdem du mir all die harten Lektionen gelernt hast, die ich lernen musste. Jetzt fühle ich mich wie eine Königin, in ihrem Luxusbett, das in Wirklichkeit ein Bus ist, aber das ist jetzt egal, durch deinen grünen, tropischen Bananen, Kokosnusspalmen und Bambusgarten rollend, und ich bin frei, frei schwebend, endlich frei von all der Schwere und dem Schmerz der alten Welt, endgültig frei. Diese Reise ist wirklich kein *Sightseeing*. Sie ist eine spirituelle Entwicklung, ein Wachsen zusammen in Liebe. Es gibt so viele Ebben und Fluten, Geschichten zu erzählen, Herausforderungen, denen du dich stellst, Brücken, die du überquerst, Durchbrüche, die du erlebst, und kostbare Seelen, die du triffst auf deinem Weg. Nach all dem, realisierst du, dass alles, was je zählte, der Moment war, der alles ist, was du hast. Gut oder schlecht. Umarme ihn, lebe ihn, ohne Wertung oder zu viel Nachdenken. Lebe ihn einfach. Und dort steht sie. Kleines, wunderschönes Mädchen, das den Schhlüssel hält.

Sapa, Vietnam, November 2023

In Indien landend

In Indien zu landen nach 10 Wochen Asien Tiefgang fühlt sich soo gut an!! Wie eine Feier. Mein Taxifahrer warf mich irgendwo im verrückten Zentrum von Varanasi raus, wo ich auf einem Motorrad runter zu den Stufen des Ganges Fluss fuhr—der heiligsten Stätte Indiens, wo du die toten Körper brennen siehst und die Pilger, wie sie im Fluss baden, der diese Gänsehaut-Atmosphäre hat, mit all den Tempeln, Zeremonien, Kerzen und Booten. Ich fühle mich hier sehr willkommen von den liebenswerten Einheimischen, die sagen, zu helfen sei gut für das Karma—sie lieben es, dir den Weg durch das lebhafte Labyrinth von eintausend Basaren, Rishkas, Fahrrädern, Motorrädern und Menschen zu zeigen, und Hasch sei gut für Kamasutra, *lol*. Obwohl sie ihren Glauben hier sehr ernst nehmen, liegt Freude in der Luft und ich fühle überhaupt nicht die Notwendigkeit, mich zu bedecken, und weniger bei 30 Grad, wie mir gesagt wurde, dass man das in Indien müsste. Kein Argument auf der Welt rechtfertigt die Notwendigkeit einer Frau, sich zu bedecken, und ein Mann nicht, und du wirst mehr Respekt dafür bekommen, wenn du bist, wer du wirklich bist, als durch eine Deklaration des Glaubens und Stigma anderer Leute. Langes oder kurzes Kleid, den Göttern ist das wirklich egal.

Varanasi, Indien, November 2023

Ich bin der meisterhafte
Verwirklicher meiner Träume

Ich bin der meisterhafte Verwirklicher meiner Träume. Das bedeutet, dass du deine Wünsche des Herzens ganz genau ausmalen musst und ohne einen einzigen Zweifel daran, sie zu empfangen, denn warum sollte dir nicht das gegeben werden, wovon du träumst, und dann gibst du sie an das Universum ab, und sie werden dir gegeben werden. Das ist das, was ich getan habe. Ich sehnte mich nach einem Platz in Goa ohne Lärm, ohne Herden von *New Age Hippies* oder Touristen in einem wunderschönen, kühlen Haus unter Palmen, mit einem großartigen Bett und mit einer Terrasse direkt am Ozean, und das ist das, was ich bekam. Es tauchte heute einfach auf, während ich am Strand entlang lief—also ein Fischer hat mich dahin gebracht, nachdem wir uns bei seiner Hütte unter Palmen am Strand unterhielten, zwischen den Fischerbooten und den Blumen, den ich so sehr liebe und wo die Einheimischen es lieben, ihr Essen mit mir zu teilen, und mich wie Familie behandeln. Ich wollte nicht in einer kleinen, halbmondförmigen, palmenbestandenen Bucht, überladen von einhundert Sonnenliegen, Hütten, Hotels und Leuten, mit eintausend Geschichten sein und mit dieser lauten Animation für Leute, die Stille nicht aushalten, das Leben nicht aushalten, sich selbst nicht aushalten können, die ein ständiges Programm brauchen, die null Verständnis für Natur haben, und alles, was ich höre von meinem Zimmer, ist das Geräusch des Ozeans. Ich musste wieder der Erde und dem Kosmos zuhören. Meine größte Inspiration. Hier gibt es nur mich und die Fischer—oft geben sie mir das Abendessen direkt vom Boot—und den weiten, offenen warmen, zauberhaften, kraftvollen, wunderschönen, Indischen Ozean. Ich musste am Ozean sein. Der Ozean ist meine Animation. Heilt meine Seele, reinigt meinen Körper, füllt mich mit Kraft, mit Leben.

Colva, Goa, Indien, November 2023

Wiedergeboren

Und es ist nach 18 Monaten, die du auf drei Kontinenten in nur einem Jahr bereist hast, eine große Mission, auf die du gestoßen wurdest und die durch die Kräfte des Universums begünstigt wurde, während du dem Kompass deines Herzens folgtest, nach 18 Leben, die du gelebt hast in nur einem Jahr, nach einem Tiefgang in all die verschiedenen Kulturen, Dimensionen und Zeiten, da ist dieser plötzliche Moment der Vollendung—und Freude beginnt durch jede einzelne deiner Zellen zu strömen und wird in dem Spiel und Lachen der Kinder reflektiert, in deinem Tanz nachts auf deiner Terrasse zum *Beat* des nahen Strandclubs unter Kokosnusspalmen in der Meeresbrise in deinem Bikini, reflektiert in den Fischerbooten, die ein Gemälde malen wie sie zusammen draußen in den roten indischen Sonnenuntergang in See stechen, eine Freude und eine Leichtherzigkeit, die du vermisst hast und niemals wieder vermissen willst und die du mit dir tragen wirst, wo auch immer du hingehst. Du bist wiedergeboren. Es ist in dem Moment, wo du all die alten Glaubenssätze verabschiedest, dass das Leben hart und schwer sei, wenn du den kosmischen *Flow* der Liebe und des Lebens entschlüsselst, den du durch deinen Körper rennend spürst. Der Moment, wo du weißt, dass du deinen eigenen Traum in jedem Moment selbst kreierst, dass du kreierst, wovon du auch immer träumst, der Moment, wo du fließt. Reitet die kosmische Welle von Liebe und Leben weiter, die immer da ist, um aufzuspringen, meine Freunde.

Colva, Goa, Indien, November 2023

Bombay Love

Ich bin froh, dass ich das Geld nicht hatte,
um im legendären Taj Mahal Palace Hotel zu
bleiben, indem das Geld, das in einem Tag
ausgegeben wird, ganz Indien aus der Armut
heben könnte, sondern dass ich dich in einem
alten, heruntergekommenen, roten, Kolonial
Fünf-Etagen-Hotel gegenüber dem Taj Mahal
am Fenster lehnend, unter dem aufsteigenden
Vollmond, in den warmen, freien, goldenen
indischen Abendhimmel hier in Bombay
blickend, küsste. Nur Liebe kann dich echt
machen. Lässt dich durch das Tor von der
Illusion in die Realität schreiten, vom Schatten
in das Licht. Lässt dich wieder zu dem werden,
was du schon immer warst. Liebe.

Bombay, Indien, November 2023

Das Leben ist ein Traum und du bist der Autor

Über die Autorin

Janet Kaufmann wurde in der ehemaligen DDR im Osten Deutschlands geboren, wo sie als Kind den Fall der Berliner Mauer miterlebte. Sie studierte Pädagogik, Psychologie und Fremdsprachen an der Universität Leipzig in Deutschland und an der Universität Aix-Marseille in Frankreich. Neben Deutsch spricht sie fließend Englisch, Französisch, Spanisch und Italienisch. Sie arbeitete als Lehrerin und Privatlehrerin in Deutschland, Russland, Italien und Ungarn sowie als Journalistin für die internationale Abteilung des deutschen MDR-Fernsehens und des französischen ARTE-Fernsehens, neben vielen anderen Jobs in Deutschland, Frankreich, Spanien, Monaco, England, Schottland und mehr, um Lebenserfahrung zu sammeln und sich ihre Reisen zu finanzieren.

Sie hat drei Bücher in den fünf Sprachen, die sie spricht, geschrieben—*Age of Liberation* (2021), *Taste of Freedom / L'Esprit de Liberté / Sabor a Libertad*

(2023) und *Like a Thrill / Wie ein Rausch / Alla corrente del vento* (2024). In ihren Büchern erzählt sie, wie sie sich auf ihrem Sprung ins Unbekannte, der sie rund um den Globus führte, von einschränkenden Glaubenssätzen und den Normen und Zwängen der Gesellschaft und Kultur befreite und viele verschiedene Länder und Kulturen kennenlernte. Sie zeigt uns, wie wir einen inneren Zustand der Freiheit, der Liebe und des Einheitsbewusstseins erreichen können, und inspiriert und ermutigt uns, ein neues Lebensmodell zu leben, das auf Freiheit, Unabhängigkeit, Kreativität und Gemeinschaft basiert, mit einem ganzheitlichen Ansatz anstatt ein konditioniertes Leben in einer kleinen Box zu führen. Ihre Bücher enthalten einzigartige Abenteuer, Inspirationen und ermutigende Botschaften, um gemeinsam neue Lebensformen zu schaffen, indem wir aus dem alten Programm von Angst, Kontrolle und Macht von oben heraustreten. Sie zeigt uns, wie wir aufsteigen, in unserer Kraft stehen und gemeinsam ein selbstbestimmtes glückliches Leben und eine neue, bessere Welt erschaffen können.

Sie begann in einem frühen Alter zu reisen und hat bis jetzt fast 60 Länder in Europa, Nord- und Südamerika, Afrika und Asien bereist. Neben ihren Reisen um die Welt lebt die Autorin heute zwischen Deutschland und Indien und engagiert sich in verschiedenen, nachhaltigen und kreativen Projekten mit der lokalen Gemeinschaft, Freunden und Familie weltweit. Als Künstlerin stellt sie ihre außergewöhnlichen Fotografien aus aller Welt in verschiedenen Orten und Galerien aus. Sie hat gerade ihren ersten eigenen Kurzfilm in Indien gedreht. Sie möchte durch ihre Literatur und Kunst und durch ihre freie und glückliche Lebensweise die Welt inspirieren und zu einem positivem Wandel beitragen.

Im Feuer Unserer Liebe
Brannten die alten Wege und die alte
Welt nieder zu Asche
In die heiligen Wasser verstreut
Wo wir Aufsteigen
Als ein Neues Kosmisches Gesetz
Göttlicher Liebe

Alla corrente del vento

Scritti da tutto il mondo che
illuminano il tuo orizzonte

Janet Kaufmann

L'unica rivoluzione che può accadere è quella
che viene dall'interno dei nostri cuori

Sommario

I. Vento del nord

Sono una artista

Sono una artista
Ho bisogno di molta quiete
Perché il mio spirito si possa riposare
nella sua nave
Su questa terra fisica
Su cui siamo venuti
Per amare di nuovo

Isola di Skye, Scozia, Ottobre 2022

Tick tack tock

Tick tack tock
Abolite tutti gli orologi
Il tempo nella cornice
Non si addice al mio nome
Terra e cielo sono la mia guida
Il sole e la luna
Illuminano la mia strada
Vivi giorno per giorno

Isola di Skye, Scozia, Settembre 2022

Parlare, parlare, parlare

Parlare, parlare, parlare
Oh tutti i discorsi della gente
Chiacchiere senza senso
Il tempo, il vicino, il primo ministro
Un'altra birra, chiacchiere senza paura
La mattina dopo
Silenzio che tace
Dov'è la tua azione?
Stupide distrazioni
Non importa il tempo
Costruiamo qualcosa di meglio

Isola di Skye, Scozia, Settembre 2022

Le anime vaganti

Noi, le anime vaganti, non viaggiamo solo per divertimento, è molto di più. Quello che a voi forse sembra una vacanza, in realtà è anche lavoro. Mentre gli altri siedono negli uffici o riempiono gli scaffali dei supermercati, noi ripristiniamo e purifichiamo le energie distorte di intere terre e popoli, colleghiamo luoghi, tempi e dimensioni e ancoriamo coscienza cosmica mentre ci espandiamo nella nostra stessa infinità, nell'amore e nell'Unità con tutto ciò che è, e di notte mi capita di andare a lavorare al pub del posto. Quindi, non è molto diverso da te e anch'io ho fatto gli scaffali del supermercato e lavori d'ufficio, ma niente più schiavitù dell'uomo per me, no! Forse non parliamo molto del nostro lavoro cosmico e la maggior parte di esso lo facciamo inconsciamente e forse lo fai anche tu, o sai dove vai nei tuoi sogni di notte?

Isola di Skye, Scozia, Settembre 2022

Oceano blu, freddo e umido

Davanti ai miei occhi, un oceano umido, freddo e blu. Oggi, onde corte, spruzzi e schiaffi sui grandi ciottoli rotondi di fronte al molo. La spiaggia è quasi sommersa. Il mare oggi è increspato e fa oscillare un paio di barche. Piccole e grandi, pescherecci blu, gialli, rossi, verdi e marroni. Alcune ondeggiano così tanto che quasi ti gira la testa. Una entra, l'altra esce. Mi chiedo che tipo di pesce abbiano pescato. Voglio andare con loro. Forse incontrerò il pescatore. Cammino lungo il molo contro una brezza tesa. Nessun'anima in giro in questo freddo lunedì sera di novembre. Dalle case colorate allineate lungo il molo escono luci fioche. Tutti sono a casa. Sono l'unico spettatore nel cinema stasera.

Isola di Skye, Scozia, Novembre 2022

Il pescatore

La magia di questo piccolo luogo esiste ancora, e li troverai se non ti precipiti in una delle attrazioni turistiche. Così siedo qui su questa piccola spiaggia rocciosa, dove i turisti di solito non si allontanano, mentre loro scattano foto dal molo e gli altri si siedono a bere nel pub e così l'ho tutta per me, con gli uccelli marini che entrano ed escono e il dolce infrangersi delle onde che cullano una manciata di barche da pesca allineate con le facciate colorate—la casetta rosa, blu, verde e gialla, ognuna con la sua storia da raccontare e così incontro il pescatore che esce con la sua barca in questa bella giornata di ottobre.

Isola di Skye, Scozia, Ottobre 2022

Ponte arcobaleno

La vita è tutta una questione di improvvisazione, di adattamento al momento sempre presente che si dispiega in un milione di possibilità diverse. È bello essere 'bloccati'. È bello non avere la mia macchina. Camminare su quella strada vuota. In una fredda ma splendida giornata di novembre. Vedere la prima neve sulle cime delle montagne. Sentire la terra sotto i miei piedi. L'energia che scorre attraverso il mio corpo. La brezza fresca sulle mie guance. Salutare le pecore al bordo della strada. Sentire il mio respiro rallentare, perché sono nella natura, in venerazione della Creazione, camminando attraverso il ponte dell'arcobaleno. La prigione della società e della cultura diventa una goccia irrilevante da qualche parte oltre l'orizzonte. È bello ricevere un passaggio da questi simpatici croati, ucraini e scozzesi e condividere l'entusiasmo della vita. È bello scendere di nuovo da quella macchina, voltarsi, vedere le nuvole che arrivano, camminare davanti a loro, verso la luce. Attraverso la pioggia, nel buio. Ritornare alla luce. Sempre di ritorno alla luce.

Isola di Skye, Scozia, Novembre 2022

Risveglio spirituale

Avrò avuto circa 16 anni quando ho scoperto e amato per la prima volta l'altro mondo, quello non fisico. In realtà, da neonati e da bambini ci siamo sempre dentro. Ricordo di essere scappata di casa per sdraiarmi supina su una collina innevata, e guardare il cielo in un deserto di bianco, fumando una sigaretta che mi dava le vertigini: uno stato che in un certo senso mi piaceva perché mi distaccava dal mondo fisico, quello che conoscevo. Le persone prendono droghe e bevono alcolici per liberarsi per un po' dalla loro dolorosa esistenza fisica, che è dolorosa quando ci disconnettiamo dallo spirito, dalla Sorgente, dalla natura, dal nostro vero sé, da ciò e da chi siamo veramente. Anch'io esageravo con l'erba e i drink, perché non ne avevo mai abbastanza di essere in quel luogo dove sentivo un senso più grande, una profondità che mancava nella nostra vita quotidiana fisica e programmata—un luogo dove mi sentivo più a casa, fino a quando, fortunatamente, sulla trentina il mio sé superiore decise di avere un risveglio spirituale invece di morire di una vita da rock 'n' roll, ed è questo che mi catapultò al mio posto, sul mio sentiero dell'anima, in un modo molto intenso ed estremo, che era la rottura di cui avevo bisogno. In termini tecnici, ha aperto i miei chakra, il terzo occhio per vedere e tutti gli altri chakra con la più grande forza vitale che scorreva attraverso di me—l'energia Kundalini, l'energia cosmica. L'apertura e l'attivazione dei tuoi centri energetici—questo è tutto ciò che un risveglio spirituale è veramente ed è ora di capirlo bene—è un'apertura dei tuoi chakra che ti riallinea alla Sorgente, alla natura, al cosmo, e niente sarà più come prima e non avrai mai più bisogno di drogarti o di bere (io non lo faccio) perché ora puoi trovarti in quello spazio sacro in modo naturale e rimanerci con un po' di sana pratica spirituale regolare, come la meditazione, l'introspezione, l'espressione della tua anima, il radicamento nella natura, l'evitare tutto ciò che è tossico—così semplice. Ora ho perso il filo di quello che volevo dire, cioè perché amo le cose che hanno un sapore e una sensazione un po' cosmica, oltre a quelle terrene che amo altrettanto—sono infatti interconnesse e mi piace sottolineare l'importanza della collegamento di entrambe nella vita quotidiana e nella società che manca e che è la ragione per cui il mondo è fuori equilibrio. Ecco perché elogio la libertà e l'amore profondo, perché amo i viaggi senza limiti e le avventure epiche, semplicemente la vita. Vivere la vita al di fuori di questa stupida scatola di cartone in cui cercano di metterti, e non sono mai stata destinata a non romperla.

Isola di Skye, Scozia, Ottobre 2022

Nuova scuola

Essendo un'insegnante di professione, non credo più nel nostro sistema scolastico e sto dubitando di volermi impegnare mai più in questa forma. Credo che l'apprendimento debba avvenire in modo naturale, senza orari, muri e cornici troppo fissi e attraverso la scoperta e l'esplorazione, anziché l'indottrinamento, per crescere bambini in grado di pensare con la propria testa, di formarsi un'opinione e di costruirsi un futuro e un modo di vivere per realizzarsi ed essere felici. Il nuovo apprendimento potrebbe avvenire sotto forma di comunità in cui gli adulti e gli anziani condividono con i bambini il loro sapere, le loro capacità, i loro doni e i loro talenti, che possono essere qualsiasi cosa, dal giardinaggio alla danza, dal canto alla costruzione, dal disegno alla meditazione, dall'equitazione alla cucina, ecc. In questo modo, l'apprendimento diventa più naturale, oltre che divertente, in tutte le diverse fasce d'età, e la comunità costruisce valori come l'amore, il rispetto, l'empatia, l'integrità e la comunione, invece di giovani insicuri e adulti infelici che competono guidati dall'ego. Ci deve essere un accesso e un'interazione diretta con diversi campi di interesse per i bambini, come l'arte, la letteratura, la filosofia, le lingue e le culture straniere, la storia, la botanica, ecc., in modo che possano scegliere e studiare da soli o insieme, invece di seguire rigidi programmi di studio creati troppo tempo fa da persone che spesso non hanno alcuna idea della vita reale e invece di essere sottoposti a una costante pressione per conseguire un rendimento. Devono avere molto spazio per non fare nulla o qualsiasi cosa desiderino fare, perché è così che nascono le grandi idee e perché siamo nati per essere liberi. Il sistema scolastico è superato se anche tu sei un visionario, se hai il coraggio di essere libero.

Isola di Skye, Scozia, Novembre 2022

Vedere il loro cuore quando apri il tuo

Non preoccuparti delle persone scortesi che non ti amano perché sei felice. E non lasciare mai che questo ti impedisca di rendere felici gli altri. Come il bevitore di whisky che ha detto di amarmi e quanto è stato bello vederlo sorridere quando ero in piedi al bar a mezzogiorno, proprio così, perché non devo mai separarmi da tutte le persone diverse, ma stare in mezzo alla vita, e perché il mio collega in cucina può essere altrettanto illuminato di quello che si dichiara apertamente tale e non devo giudicare chi e cosa io stessa non sono, ma vedere l'uguaglianza dei nostri cuori invece delle differenze superficiali e devo riunire tutti, questo è ciò che amo. Come il ragazzo che ha tentato invano di fare l'autostop nello stesso punto in cui l'ho fatto io oggi e naturalmente l'ho invitato a venire con l'autostop che ho fatto io stesso e come questo lo ha reso felice, dato che il conducente stava andando proprio dove lui aveva cercato di arrivare per tutto il giorno—questo mi ha reso felice di vederlo felice e anche il conducente era felice perché non aveva parlato con nessuno oggi e così il mio amico irlandese con cui sono andato a fare una passeggiata oggi e quello scozzese, che incontrerò domani. Rendere felice l'altro, qualunque sia il suo credo, la sua origine o il suo status, e vedere che siamo tutti un'unica famiglia è la cosa più bella che ho imparato soprattutto nei miei viaggi e immergendomi in tutti i tipi di ambienti e culture diverse e c'è sempre la possibilità di rendere felice qualcuno, anche se si tratta di uno straniero che è là fuori sulla strada proprio come te e non giudicare mai una persona dal suo aspetto, ma vedere il loro cuore quando apri il tuo.

Isola di Skye, Scozia, Ottobre 2022

Metti il tuo amore in qualcosa di più Grande

Possiamo amare tante cose. Il mio vicino di casa, il gatto del mio vicino, mia madre, tua figlia, il mio amico, lo straniero per strada che ricambia il mio sorriso. Possiamo amare le donne, gli uomini, i bambini e gli anziani, gli animali e le piante, le rocce, le stelle, il sole, la pioggia, il vento. Ciò che amiamo è una parte di noi stessi. Sento l'amore per il vento e per il cosmo in ogni cellula del mio corpo. Mi rende più grande di quello che sono. L'amore si espande. Devo fare sesso con ciò che amo? Sì e no. Il sesso potrebbe cambiare quel legame. Quell'amicizia. L'amore è etereo e il sesso è fisico e sì, possiamo combinare le due cose, ma solo se c'è amore. Quando diventa una dipendenza, allora l'amore non è più libero o dobbiamo lasciare che l'amore fluisca? Ci sono così tanti stadi e profondità diverse dell'amore e credo che se si tratta di un vero amore profondo, bisogna lasciarlo fluire, fondersi e ascendere insieme. Se si tratta di un amore di amicizia, credo che non valga la pena di condividerlo a livello fisico, questo tema che induce costantemente a confusione e che porta a relazioni aperte, a tradimenti e a bugie, oppure conoscete una comune hippie degli anni '70 che è diventata felice per sempre ? Mentre si è sballati, sì, è bello, ma le cose sembrano diverse il giorno dopo. Perché avere una relazione se allo stesso tempo si vogliono altri partner? Perché non possiamo essere semplicemente amici? Non è forse una codipendenza, non essere in grado di stare con o senza l'altro? Credo che ci siano infinite forme di vivere l'amore, anche nelle amicizie maschio-femmina che possiamo estendere, creare qualcosa insieme. Metti il tuo amore in qualcosa di più Grande.

Isola di Skye, Scozia, Novembre 2022

Festa di Halloween

Mi dispiace, non vengo alla tua festa
di Halloween
Penso che il tuo aspetto è strano
Non lo trovo divertente
Sto sveglia di notte e scarico poesie
E tu pensi che io sia strana
Non è divertente
Portiamo solo nomi
Le stelle ti conoscono meglio

Isola di Skye, Scozia, Novembre 2022

Tra i mondi

Alcune delle innumerevoli cose che ho imparato nei miei viaggi in molti paesi, anni ed esperienze diverse sono che spostarmi da un luogo all'altro fa parte della mia natura umana, e che se mai mi stabilissi sarebbe solo per pochi mesi fino a quando mi sposterei verso il prossimo luogo o la prossima avventura, invece di fare della mia casa il mio castello controllato dal mondo materiale, collezionando e consumando sempre più cose che non mi servono nella vita o diventando troppo grassa e pigra nelle mie routine e zone di comfort. Se dovessi stabilirmi, non sarebbe mai più in una piccola scatola di cemento, perché appena apro gli occhi desidero mettere i piedi sulla madre terra, vedere l'orizzonte e camminare verso il sole. Ho anche imparato che se le persone non ti integrano o le porte non si aprono per te nel posto in cui vivi, o se non ti sei fatto dei veri amici, è ora di andare avanti. Tuttavia, nessun luogo al mondo potrà mai sostituire la tua casa, la tua scelta di incarnazione, la tua terra, dove sei nato e cresciuto. Questo non significa che dobbiamo essere legati a quel luogo per sempre, perché il vero amore non conosce attaccamento, né alle persone, né ai luoghi, né alle cose. Possiamo vivere in luoghi diversi e goderceli, contrariamente a quanto la società ci dice di essere prigionieri del nostro lavoro, della nostra casa, delle nostre cose, dei nostri circoli, dei nostri orari, del nostro tempo e del nostro luogo in una cornice. Un concetto ormai antiquato che si addice solo a chi non ha mai assaporato la libertà.

Isola di Skye, Scozia, Novembre 2022

La mia capricciosa, bellissima Scozia

La mia capricciosa, bellissima Scozia
Non ci resta molto tempo
Dolce malinconia del nord solitario
Attraverso di te ho guardato negli angoli
più profondi della mia anima
La tua bellezza aspra e frastagliata
Mi ha confortato nei giorni più bui
Per i coraggiosi
A trovare la luce

Isola di Skye, Scozia, Dicembre 2022

Autobus scosso e rumoroso

Stendo il mio corpo stanco per dormire sui
quattro sedili posteriori
Guardando le catene montuose coperte di neve
passandomi, sciogliendosi in un cielo bianco
Portami, portami lontano
L'autobus scosso e rumoroso mi culla nel sonno
Mi sveglierò in un altro luogo
Con una nuova vita
Continua a cavalcare le onde

Isola di Skye, Scozia, Dicembre 2022

II. Verso ovest

Rio, Downtown!

Ascolto la bella musica del pianoforte dal piano di sotto che suona un concerto a tempo della pioggia tiepida che sgocciola sul mio terrazzo, mentre sono sdraiata nel mio letto all'Hotel Americano, che non è affatto americano, ma molto brasiliano, e le mille immagini colorate della giornata mi passano per la mente come una ebrezza, così come la giornata è stata una ebrezza beata. Il mio primo giorno in Brasile, a Rio de Janeiro, e contrariamente alle voci degli altri e del turista americano alla reception che diceva che Rio era pericolosa e che ti avrebbero derubato subito, mi sono buttata nelle strade, nel diluvio, nei fuochi d'artificio, nella pienezza della vita. Non nel famoso quartiere di Copacabana o Ipanema, dove ho cancellato l'albergo all'ultimo minuto, ma nel vero *downtown*, dove vive la gente di Rio de Janeiro. *Oh Gesù, che bênção foi ser pobre!* Ho camminato per le strade e non ho sentito alcun pericolo, contrariamente all'avvertimento dell'americano alla reception, che pensa di essere migliore dei brasiliani e solo perché deruba la gente—lavora nella finanza—non significa che debba essere derubata anch'io! Ognuno crea la propria esperienza! Li ho visti, gli abitanti di Rio de Janeiro, e mi hanno sorriso e mi sono sentita benvenuta—bella gente, gente gentile—ho visto i loro cuori e hanno toccato il mio. C'è così tanta bellezza nel mix di cultura indigena, africana ed europea di questo continente, e sembrano leggeri di cuore, con la musica che arriva da ogni angolo. Samba, reggaeton e altra grande musica ad alto volume e ho visto una brillante arte di strada. Sono nel centro storico, nel cuore della città con tutte le feste di strada—anche qui molte persone dormono per strada e ci sono molti problemi di povertà e droga. Ho sentito gli spari dalle favelas, ma così è la vita—meglio che vivere in una bolla e sedersi in un bar noioso con i turisti in un hotel snob di Copacabana. Preferisco essere qui, nel centro della vita, con la gente, li amo tutti! Vedrò anche

Ipanema e Copacabana e amerò anche loro, proprio come i brasiliani amano le loro spiagge e domani scalerò la Montagna di Zucchero e ora devo dormire, con il mio uccellino Toukan di gemma che mi sorride e mi ha affascinato quando l'ho visto al mercato di strada—anche la foresta pluviale mi chiama! L'avventura alle porte di casa mia! Sono in Sud America e non potrei essere più felice!

Rio de Janeiro, Brasile, Gennaio 2023

Ebbrezza di Rio

Quattro giorni a Rio sembrano una vita intera in qualsiasi altra parte del mondo! Sono così innamorata di questa città più bella del mondo e della sua gente, del suo stile di vita, della sua gioia di vivere, della sua follia, dei suoi contrasti e „Oh Dio mio", della sua musica! Samba, bossa nova, reggae...! La vita qui accade per strada e tutto è un'improvvisazione o un'avventura e anche se dovrei essere stanca, mi sento piena di energia. Anche se non mi piace molto la vita di città, qui è diverso, come se tutti fossero uniti come una grande famiglia in questa vita pazza. La gente accende un fuoco in mezzo alla strada per cucinare qualcosa in una scatola di latta e mangiare sul marciapiede, perché no! Qui vendono le migliori Caipirinha a ogni angolo di strada e costano solo 50 centesimi! Poiché non mi piace l'alcol, bevo sempre acqua di cocco direttamente da una noce di cocco e da quando sono qui mangio un sacco di frutta esotica—ho già perso un po' di peso. Qui si balla molto e la vita in generale sembra così leggera, infatti ogni giorno sembra una festa! Stavo per andare a letto, ma i tamburi per strada sono così forti che non riesco a resistere.

Rio de Janeiro, Brasile, Gennaio 2023

Brasile

Hmm Brasile
Mi ricorderò di te per l'odore del tuo delizioso
caffè che sa di montagne verdi e lussureggianti
in mille sfumature di verde che si fondono con il
mare color smeraldo
Per il tuo meraviglioso mix di persone felici di
tutti i colori
Per la tua samba, la bossa nova e il sertanejo
Per i tuoi frutti e fiori esotici
Per il tuo ipnotico ritmo di tamburi
Per le persone che sono venute da lontano su
barche di legno molto tempo fa
Per la tua esuberante abbondanza
Per la tua follia
Per la tua *beleza*
Per il tuo grande e prezioso cuore

Costa Verde, Brasile, Gennaio 2023

Vento portami via

Così ho frequentato alcuni abitanti di questo villaggio dall'atmosfera hippie, che mi hanno reso partecipe dei loro *asados* quotidiani — barbecue sudamericano e sessioni di musica nella casa di El Barba — poeta e artista rivoluzionario di 84 anni, dove gli spiriti liberi si incontrano e si scambiano idee sul mondo e un sacco di tango, fado, murga, candombe, choclo, son, salsa, bossa nova... . Che piacere! Ora mi lascio portare alla corrente del vento. Sii libero e selvaggio come un cavallo uruguaiano.

Rocha, Uruguay, Gennaio 2023

Uruguay

E imparai a fluire
Gracias Uruguay
País del Río de los pajaros pintados
River river
Water water
Mar y Sol
Ora fluire

Rocha, Uruguay, Gennaio 2023

El camino

Mi sono lasciata trasportare in questo viaggio
assolutamente brillante, il più bello della mia
vita fino ad ora, attraverso il Sud America, da
sola. Dalla prima parte in Brasile, che è stata
bellissima ma un po' brusca dal caldo tropicale,
dalle tante zanzare, dal rumore, da una notte di
malattia e molte altre brevi e dal mio telefono
che è caduto dalla barca in fondo al mare color
smeraldo ed è stato recuperato dopo 24 ore da un
sommozzatore locale, che si dice possa trovare
ogni cosa—ovviamente senza attrezzatura—e
con le mie SIM inglesi e tedesche salvate—ma il
messaggio era chiaro—il viaggio si è trasformato
in una corsa brillante, intensa e veloce, con tante
mosse imprevedibili e avventure per imparare
a surfare le onde alte che ti danno quel brivido,
che ti ricordano come dovrebbe essere la vita
il più delle volte: come un'estasi e non come
un sonno o una lotta. Nel momento in cui ho
abbandonato tutti i miei piani e ho smesso
di usare internet sul mio telefono per trovare

posti per dormire o dove andare dopo—nel momento in cui mi sono arresa al flusso—le porte si sono aperte ovunque andassi, con incontri speciali e connessioni lungo la strada che mi hanno portato da un posto all'altro—un passo porta al successivo—principio geniale ma spesso ignorato della vita, per abbracciare nient'altro che il momento presente, senza aspettative e senza troppi piani. In questo modo, il cammino—*el camino*—si è aperto da solo, camminandolo. Brillante principio universale non solo di questo viaggio, ma della vita, che dispiega la sua magia quando abbiamo poche aspettative e viviamo il momento. È così che sono finita nella casetta dei miei sogni, dove mi trovo attualmente, che non costa quasi nulla nella *Sierra di Cordoba*, nel cuore dell'Argentina, la vera, autentica Argentina. Non ci sono turisti a chilometri di distanza. Si riversano tutti nella costosa e turistica Patagonia. Qui ci sono ancora i negozi all'angolo di una volta, dove il cibo viene confezionato da loro stessi in piccole quantità e tutto è biologico e gustosissimo. In ogni negozio in cui sono entrata, la gente ha iniziato a conversare con me: qui sono incredibilmente amichevoli e accoglienti, l'esatto contrario di come ho conosciuto i *Porteños*, gli abitanti di Buenos Aires. È meraviglioso vedere lo spirito di comunità e la vita nella sua semplicità e bellezza, quando il capitalismo non ha ancora permeato la società e rovinato le cose belle della vita, quando l'amore e l'unione guidano le persone invece dell'avidità e dell'egoismo. Qui la gente sembra davvero felice e le uscite e la musica hanno un ruolo importante nella vita quotidiana, ovunque e sempre, in Sud America. I negozi chiudono a mezzanotte e gli argentini vanno a letto molto tardi e, come in Uruguay, guidano auto d'epoca e amano bere il loro *Mate*—la bevanda locale a base di erbe—insieme, che è una parte importante dell'identità argentina. Il casetta in cui mi trovo attualmente è in mezzo alla natura pura e si trova sulla roccia più antica della terra—sì, si estende anche all'interno della casa — posso toccarla dal mio letto perché il mio nuovo amico Marcos, un tipo cool che ha girato il mondo prima di costruire questo piccolo rifugio qui che condivide con i visitatori, ha integrato lo spirito del paesaggio. Si trova su un ruscello sotterraneo, che regala sogni vividi e colorati, dice. A pochi passi c'è il grande fiume selvaggio, dove la gente del posto fa il bagno e che ha modellato il paesaggio con bellissime piscine in cui nuotare e persino spiagge. Di notte sento solo gli uccelli e il concerto dei grilli mentre guardo il cielo stellato mozzafiato — la natura — tornare da dove siamo venuti, dove tutto sembra ricco e divino, al di là dell'illusione del tempo.

Mina Clavero, Argentina, Gennaio 2023

Girare liberamente

Mi piacerebbe girare il mondo per sempre. Amo il movimento, i cambiamenti di paesaggio, le particolarità delle persone e delle culture, i cambiamenti di cibo, flora, fauna e clima. I sorrisi e i cuori aperti delle persone rimangono gli stessi ovunque io vada. Mi piace seguire i fiumi attraverso le valli e le catene montuose che si estendono verso il mare, attraversare gli oceani, saltare da un'isola all'altra, al di là dell'ignoto. A volte rimango ferma in un luogo per una ragione. Rifletto su me stesso e sul cammino e guardo le stelle un po' più a lungo. Vedrò un'astronave?

Da qualche parte in Argentina, Gennaio 2023

Un mondo unico

Chiunque mi abbia detto di temere l'estraneo, l'immenso, l'altro, l'ignoto, era un bugiardo. Il tuo mondo è il mio mondo e il mio mondo è il tuo mondo. Non c'è niente di più bello che condividere il mio pranzo di oggi in questa cucina pubblica della città con la gente del posto, i bambini, gli anziani, i viaggiatori—uno di quei momenti speciali del viaggio. Ho mangiato la migliore trota del lago Titicaca al mondo. Qui mangiano molto bene, si dorano i denti, si vestono molto bene e sono molto dolci, ma chiamano la Bolivia un paese del terzo mondo perché si riempiono il c*lo con i soldi solo per loro stessi. Guardate chi è più felice. Più viaggio, più mi sento parte del tutto. Le distanze e le differenze sono solo un'illusione del mondo fisico che qualcuno ha inventato per paura. Non nel mio mondo. Il nostro mondo. Le persone qui non mi trattano in modo diverso perché non vedo in loro un altro. Vedo la bellezza. Vedo amore. Ho viaggiato con pochi soldi senza preoccuparmi di quanto mi rimaneva —anche le preoccupazioni sono per gli ansiosi. Viaggiare ti rende ricco dentro. Per sempre.

Copacabana, Lago Titicaca, Bolivia, Febbraio 2023

Unire i mondi

Machu Picchu era chiuso da mesi e anche le guide turistiche peruviane mi avevano detto solo due settimane fa che era chiuso a tempo indeterminato e che non era possibile viaggiare in Perù a causa dei tumulti politici — dicevano che non avrebbe aperto fino ad aprile. Non ho visto nessuna manifestazione e sorprendentemente hanno riaperto Machu Picchu due giorni fa, quando ho comprato un biglietto, che di solito sono esauriti con mesi di anticipo, e ho praticamente avuto Machu Picchu tutta per me. Se avessi ascoltato gli altri, non sarei mai venuta in Perù. Invece ho ascoltato il mio intuito che mi diceva di andare semplicemente e il mio viaggio attraverso il lago Titicaca e le montagne è stato facile e speciale, come se fosse stato facilitato — sì, è così che è stato/è l'intero viaggio in Sud America, perché? Perché ho seguito il mio cuore ed è così che si aprono le porte. Perché tante persone vogliono visitare Machu Picchu? Per spuntarla dalla loro lista di cose da fare? Odio questa espressione, ma è anche una foto brillante se si posa accanto ad essa. Perché sono venuta a Machu Picchu? Perché ho sentito la chiamata. Unire mondi e dimensioni. Non sono una turista, sono una viaggiatrice, una esploratrice e sono una figlia del cosmo, come lo siamo tutti, che lo ricordi o no.

Machu Picchu, Perù, Febbraio 2023

Miracolo cosmico

Che palle! Perché solo un giorno prima della mia scalata di Machu Picchu dovevo ammalarmi di diarrea per aver mangiato questo ipnotico frutto giallo della foresta pluviale a me sconosciuto che produce 'pulizia del corpo', mi dissero in seguito, diarrea per essere giusti! Così, naturalmente, salgo al mio Machu Picchu, comunque dopo aver viaggiato per 10.000 miglia per arrivarci—abbastanza esausta e stanca per il magico frutto giallo e mi emoziono quando mi avvicino al sito—a causa delle mie condizioni fisiche o è Machu Picchu che mi travolge? Stupefatta, mi aggiro per il sito, incrociando piccoli gruppi di turisti che vengono bombardati di informazioni dalla loro guida e pensando tra me che non riuscirei mai ad assorbire tutte queste informazioni, così mi soffermo per un po' intorno al tempio centrale del sole—qui sento qualcosa di forte e ipnotico—e dopo un po' mi sposto, ma torno e rimango ancora un po' in quel luogo speciale, finché una delle guardie mi nota e mi chiede se voglio meditare nel tempio rituale degli sciamani, che si trova di fronte al tempio del sole e che normalmente non è aperto ai turisti e che, surriscaldato dal sole Inca, è proprio il luogo in cui ho bisogno di stare, così mi conduce segretamente nel tempio segreto dove mi siedo all'ombra degli enormi blocchi di pietra e il mio corpo si sente sollevato e inizio a respirare, respirare, respirare e lì accade: la mia coscienza si apre alle dimensioni superiori e inferiori e a tutte le dimensioni e a tutti i tempi—il passato e il futuro sono qui ora. Ricevo le energie e i segreti cosmici attraverso il mio chakra della corona, nel mio corpo fino alla radice nella terra e viceversa—dalla mia radice fino al cielo e unisco ieri, oggi, domani e per sempre. Questo è l'inizio della nuova era. È qui e ora. Io sono ogni momento.

Machu Picchu, Perù, Febbraio 2023

Cittadino del mondo

Tu cambia casa ogni pochi giorni o settimane. Proprio come quello che mangi, che cambia a seconda dei luoghi in cui viaggi. Mangi frutta e altre cose strane che non hai mai visto prima. Non ti importa se a volte bevi il caffè istantaneo freddo, mangi con le mani sul letto perché non hai un tavolo e ti piace perché ti senti libera mentre guardi fuori dalla finestra della tua piccola e bella pensione che ti costa molto meno dell'affitto di una casa a casa tua e guardi le colline e lo slogan—*Viva el Perù*—che è scritto lì mentre il sole tramonta lentamente e pacificamente sui tetti rossi di Cuzco e ti senti un cittadino del mondo. Non sei sicuro di doverti fermare ora—a volte vuoi che questo viaggio non finisca mai—potresti andare avanti all'infinito, ogni volta più coraggiosa, più saggia, più calma e più felice e sai che a volte il tuo corpo si stanca e lo lasci essere stanco—non vai di fretta solo quando è necessario e sai quando devi fare uno sforzo e se a volte devi correre, e se perdi ancora l'unico autobus, ti dici 'Fa***lo' e ti piace **essere** ferma e non sai esattamente cosa sia meglio: l'eccitazione di movimento —osservando i paesaggi che cambiano, le altitudini, i climi, la vegetazione e i tratti e i costumi delle persone o rimanendo più a lungo in un luogo che ti diventa familiare quando scopri i suoi segreti a uno sguardo più approfondito, ma sai che è brillante, la vita. E la preoccupazione più grande quando pensi a cosa metterti oggi è decidere il rosso o il verde, perché tutto quello che ti serve sta in un piccolo zaino e se manca qualcosa, lo compri per strada e quando il tuo cappello preferito viene spazzato via dal vento sulla nave su cui ti trovi, lo lasci andare e lo dai al mare argentato del *Rio de la Plata* e sei fermamente convinta che ne troverai uno ancora migliore. E il cappello nuovo che compri in Bolivia lo lasci a chi lo troverà in Perù, perché in Colombia non è più adatto al tuo stile e a Panama ne troverai uno ancora più bello. E a volte si fa nuove amicizie lungo la strada e le si saluta e non sai se le rivedrai mai, ma sai per certo che le amerai per sempre.

Cuzco, Perù, Febbraio 2023

Cuzco

Questo viaggio è così brillante perché non è limitato dal tempo o da altre convinzioni. Il mondo è il mio salotto. A volte mi sembra di volare, come il condor sudamericano che volteggia in alto al suono del flauto peruviano nella scena di sottofondo e il mio cuore trabocca di gioia.

Cuzco, Perù, Febbraio 2023

Le deviazioni sono i percorsi migliori

C***o. L´ ho capito. L'avventura non è sempre liscia e confortevole. A volte diventa turbolento e difficile e i piani vanno in frantumi. Gli itinerari prendono direzioni diverse e le esperienze paradisiache possono trasformarsi inaspettatamente in esperienze infernali. Segue sempre un'epifania, una di quelle che non ci si aspettava. Si può ottenere l'audacia e la saggezza di un'intera vita in un solo giorno. Quel giorno ti scuote, senti l'avventura scorrere in ogni tua cellula e quelle che sembravano le peggiori 48 ore della tua vita si trasformano di colpo in un'esperienza eroica che ti fa crescere per tutta la vita, che ti fa sentire più vivo di un'intera città che va al lavoro e torna a casa da 20 anni facendo la stessa cosa, ma io sono qui fuori a capire che non c'è linearità e non c'è tempo. Le cose possono di colpo iniziare a vorticare e a girare come pazze e tutto quello che devi fare è allacciare la cintura di sicurezza e stringere i denti. Ieri all'aeroporto mi hanno negato l'uscita dal Perù perché si sono dimenticati di darmi un timbro d'ingresso all'arrivo, due settimane fa, nonostante fossi passata attraverso il confine ufficiale. (A volte in Sud America ti chiedono se vuoi passare attraverso il confine ufficiale o non ufficiale.) Sono cose che succedono e ciò che non era colpa mia non poteva essere risolto né dalla polizia, né dall'ufficio centrale per l'immigrazione di Lima, né dall'ambasciata tedesca, che non erano in grado di aiutarmi perché sono troppo bloccati dalla loro burocrazia e hanno perso la capacità di pensare in modo flessibile e orientato alla soluzione, perché sono controllati da leggi insensate, dall'ordine e dal potere dall'alto, che spesso trasformano le persone in robot insensibili e stupidi, dipendenti dai loro telefoni, bloccati nella matrice e resi insensibili, per cui ho dovuto andare a cercare una soluzione da sola, invece di rimanere per sempre nel paese del Perù. Sono tornata indietro di più di 1000 miglia fino al posto di controllo di frontiera dove ero entrata per ottenere il timbro, per una ridicola goccia d'inchiostro. Ho viaggiato in *colectivo*—mini van o auto che raccolgono persone sulla strada—per tornare a Puno, cosa che in Sudamerica significa rimanere bloccati per un´eternità sulle strade, affidarsi a *colectivos* sporchi e rumorosi, nel caso oggi si facciano vedere e con mia grande sorpresa mi hanno regalato un viaggio affascinante attraverso la parte più panoramica delle Ande, dove i turisti non arrivano quasi mai. Non dimenticherò mai le immagini dei branchi di lama sugli altopiani deserti, dei fenicotteri nelle lagune gelate, l'ipnotizzante maestoso vulcano Misti con la sua cima innevata all'orizzonte che sovrasta tutto e con il mio cuore e la mia mente che si aprono come mai prima d'ora sulla bellezza del pianeta e fluttuano in beatitudine nel viaggio della mia vita che non vorrei mai scambiare per nessun lusso al mondo in una vacanza con cocktail in piscina in un paese del sud senza emozioni—per una bugia venduta di un'illusione, per un'immagine di un paese che non è vera. Preferisco la vita reale e amo l'avventura. Siate coraggiosi, amici miei. Siate liberi. Siate forti.

Da qualche parte in Perù, Febbraio 2023

Come una ebrezza

Speciale, intensa, emozionante,
A volte dolce come un caffè colombiano in un
pomeriggio dorato nella piazza centrale di
una dolce e colorata cittadina tra le montagne
colombiane,
Altre volte estasiante, come ai margini di una
notte brasiliana.
A volte vorrei che questo viaggio,
Questa ebbrezza,
non finisse mai.
Decido dove andare e cosa fare in momenti,
da un'ispirazione, da un'immagine o da un
incontro.
È come se viaggiassi ad alta velocità,
completamente in flusso e prendessi questa
uscita 29 che non sapevo esistesse e che ti porta
In paradiso.

Da qualche parte a Panama, Marzo 2023

Paradiso nascosto

Sono in paradiso, un paradiso nascosto. Arrivare qui è stato puro istinto e avventura, come sempre. Non ho mai visto questo posto menzionato da nessuna parte prima d'ora, ed è per questo che è così bello e sembra che io sia l'unico turista qui, lontano dai pochi luoghi turistici sovraffollati e troppo costosi di Panama—non ho mai capito perché la gente vuole andare dove vanno tutti. Posso scegliere tra la spiaggia privata di fronte a casa mia e la spiaggia principale, dove i giovani si ritrovano e fanno festa: è quella sensazione caraibica assolutamente meravigliosa. Qui sembra tutto molto tranquillo rispetto ad alcuni luoghi piuttosto malfamati che ho visto, soprattutto a Panama City, ma mi è stato detto che in tutto il paese operano bande di narcotrafficanti. Non c'è nulla di cui preoccuparsi qui, ho una protezione speciale da parte della polizia e mi sto facendo viziare dalla famiglia dove ho affittato una bella camera vista mare che si affaccia sulle spiagge di sabbia bianca e zuccherina incorniciate da palme da cocco, con una gustosa cucina caraibica, pesce freschissimo e gite in barca. Tuttavia, come sempre, non mi fido di nessuno. Il poliziotto mi ha chiesto il numero di telefono e l'hotel della famiglia in cui alloggio, che sembra benestante, anche se è vuoto nonostante sia alta stagione. Non mi importa: mi sto solo dondolando sulla mia amaca qui, dove l'unico rumore che sento è quello del vento che soffia sul mare, della musica latina ad alto volume che esce dalle case e dei buffi versi dei pappagalli. La gente del posto si avvicina a me con curiosità e cordialità. Parla la loro lingua e vai dove nessuno va.

La Guaiara, Panama, Marzo 2023

Fuori nella giungla

Credo che vivere nella giungla—vivere nella natura—come fanno ancora innumerevoli tribù indigene in tutto il mondo, compresa la Costa Rica, richieda una forma di intelligenza superiore, un'abilità elaborata nell'osservare il proprio ambiente, una profonda comprensione e conoscenza della natura e delle sue specie, della sopravvivenza in sé con una interazione piena di senso, equilibrata e creativa con l'ambiente naturale che cambia ogni giorno nella sua geniale creazione divina—e vivere nella natura non è in alcun modo più primitivo, come viene falsamente pubblicizzato, che vivere uno stile di vita occidentale condizionato in una piccola scatola, facendo ogni giorno le stesse cose che riducono l'intelligenza complessa e fanno rimpicciolire le capacità cognitive, poiché richiedono un pensiero e un'azione poco creativi, quando ci tagliamo fuori dalla nostra più bella, più geniale maestra e madre. Madre Natura. E si torna alla civiltà e si balla ancora di più.

Manzanillo, Costa Rica, Marzo 2023

III. Terra d'origine

Di ritorno a casa

Non riesco a credere di essere tornata viva—di nuovo in una Germania organizzata e ordinata, il contrasto potrebbe essere più grande? No! Sono le sfide che ti fanno crescere e dopo aver viaggiato per 3 mesi attraverso il Sud e il Centro America da sola, mi sento un Gigante. Questo viaggio è stato incredibile e impegnativo fino all'ultimo minuto. Ho dovuto affrontare e superare le mie paure e i miei limiti molte volte—niente è più bello una volta che l'hai fatto—e mi sono mossa costantemente al di fuori della mia zona di comfort. È ciò che mi fa sentire viva, dove sono più nel mio elemento, dove la vita sembra un brivido, e una volta scossi, ci si risveglia per sempre. L'avventura è la migliore droga del mondo! Parte di questo è stato anche il fatto che mi sono ammalata alcune volte, ho dovuto affrontare sfide fisiche dovute a climi, altezze e diete diverse, mi sono infilata in veicoli sporchi e maleodoranti, notti e giorni di viaggio—che non sempre sembravano tali—verso l'ignoto.

Ho affrontato enormi creature della giungla, ho dormito in cento letti diversi, ho mangiato cose molto deliziose e molto schifose e ho continuato a camminare. Ho perso voli, mi è stata negata l'uscita, mi sono stati tolti oggetti personali e sono stata quasi arrestata per disobbedienza alle autorità. Mi agito sempre di nuovo come un'adolescente selvaggia per le ingiustizie dovute alla mancanza di cuore e di empatia, per le persone che si comportano come robot che seguono ciecamente regole severe invece di essere umano e continuerò a dire chiaramente ciò che penso e più dura sarà la punizione, più amerò—è per questo che siamo qui, chi si ricorda di questo? Chi ricorda se stesso? Per ricordare ancora di più, andrò sempre più lontano, desidero esplorare gli angoli più inesplorati del mondo, i più remoti della mia stessa anima e troverò persone che guardano, mangiano, parlano in modo diverso e che amano ugualmente. Continuerò a ridere del sistema, continuerò a insegnare ciò che conta e insegnerò ai bambini a non avere paura e ad avere una mente aperta. Continuerò a difendere i miei diritti e le mie convinzioni, continuerò a vivere l'avventura senza limiti, la libertà, l'unità, la creatività fuori dagli schemi e continuerò a scriverne e a catturarne la bellezza in scatti da tutto il mondo. Nata per vivere, nata per amare.

Monti Metalliferi, Germania, Marzo 2023

Terra d'origine

Nel corso del tuo viaggio alla fine scoprirai che nessun paese è veramente migliore di un altro per quanto riguarda i sistemi e la maggior parte delle cose ha lati positivi e negativi, ma il paese che spesso ci frustra di più è quello in cui siamo nati, ma ricorda che è stata la tua libera scelta quella di incarnarti lì e questo per un motivo. Dopo aver vagato e dopo ciò che abbiamo visto e imparato in diverse parti del mondo, potremmo tornare al nostro luogo di nascita o a un altro luogo dell'anima e cambiare le cose dove è più necessario, creare ciò che vogliamo vedere invece di cercarlo altrove. Ciò che è fresco e nuovo sembra sempre migliore, ma solo a prima vista, e scoprirai che i problemi che affrontiamo sono simili ovunque nel mondo e che il nostro mondo dei sogni non esiste se non lo creiamo noi, per questo siamo venuti qui. Possiamo saltare da un posto all'altro e vivere in luoghi diversi, il che rende la vita molto più eccitante, ma non perderti mai il tuo qui e ora. Madre Natura è grande ovunque e proprio nel luogo in cui ti trovi. Annaffiala, rispettala, proteggila, amala, danza su di lei. Insieme, famiglia dell'anima.

Monti Metalliferi, Germania, Dicembre 2023

Spazio immenso, divino e vasto

Mentre guardo dalla finestra, conto nove alberi di mele, tre di ciliegie, tre di prugne e tre di pere in piena fioritura nel nostro giardino. Un giovane gatto tigrato arancione si aggira tra l'erba alta a caccia nel sole dorato della sera. Il silenzio pacifico è interrotto solo da alcuni uccelli che cinguettano. Là fuori c'è un immenso spazio divino da riempire con dolce dolce vita.

Monti Metalliferi, Germania, Aprile 2023

Natura, sei la mia casa preziosa

Natura, sei la mia casa preziosa
Il mio rifugio da quando ho saputo scappare
Lontano da castelli dorati e dalla società in
una scatola
Non sono qui per dipingere a colori la
tua scatola
Seguo il flusso del fiume
Il soffio del vento
Là dove la vita cresce
Nel mio mondo libero a colori

Monti Metalliferi, Germania, Aprile 2023

Pioggia d'aprile

Pioggia d'Aprile
Hai lavato via il mio dolore
Mi sono seduta su un treno vuoto
E la natura non era più spoglia
Ho liberato i miei pensieri da vecchie catene
Viaggiare mi ha reso di nuovo libera

Sassonia, Germania, Aprile 2023

Spirito comunitario

Una società orientata al denaro e all'egoismo uccide qualsiasi spirito comunitario. Secondo la mia esperienza, più la gente è povera, più la comunità è grande. Ho sperimentato la comunità tra le persone nella sua forma più pura in Sud America e in Africa ed era anche il luogo in cui le persone sembravano più felici anche se avevano meno. So che anche in Europa c'è uno spirito comunitario, ma secondo me è difficile da trovare. Non è un segreto che condividere e creare qualcosa insieme renda più felici che avere tutto per sé. Esiste una serie di nuove forme sperimentali di comunità che stanno emergendo come controreazione alla totale mancanza di spirito comunitario nelle nostre culture occidentali. Mi riferisco ai cosiddetti circoli *New Age* o *Family*, come si definiscono, che spesso si separano dal resto perché si considerano diversi o spesso addirittura migliori, motivo per cui li respingo e anche perché spesso assumono un'altra forma di estremo. Possiamo ricordare che cos'è la vera comunità? Che è semplicemente preoccuparsi del vicino e avere una coscienza della società nel suo complesso, creare qualcosa insieme e completarsi a vicenda, piuttosto che competere con l'altro o compiacere l'altro, con questo strano bisogno di non distinguersi, piuttosto che essere se stessi e liberare il proprio potenziale più alto per il bene di tutti, e piuttosto che inseguire ciecamente il denaro? Credo che siamo qui per creare una vita basata sulla creatività, sulla sostenibilità, sulla libertà e sull'indipendenza dal vecchio sistema di potere e di controllo, insieme alla nostra tribù dell'anima, che non significa nient'altro che i nostri veri amici, le persone con cui ci si trova sulla stessa lunghezza d'onda, Connessioni che si basano sul cuore e non sull'ego con un'agenda, insieme ai visionari, a coloro che ricordano che la vita è il dono più grande sulla terra e che siamo qui per viverla pienamente—non per esistere, non per sopravvivere, non per funzionare, non per comprare, ma per prosperare. Insieme.

Monti Metalliferi, Germania, Marzo 2023

Camminare con le stagioni

Forse non mi fermo mai perché non dovrei fermarmi. Perché sono una vera nomade e uno spirito libero nel cuore, perché non è nella mia natura rinchiudermi in una piccola scatola di cemento e muovermi tra la via della spesa e il lavoro—sola e infelice come una schiava di un mondo di soldi, che esegue ordini e doveri e ha paura di uscire dalle linee?! Forse perché le mie convinzioni sono illimitate come lo è il mondo, i cui confini sono artificiali e non costituiscono mai un ostacolo per un vero avventuriero. Forse la mia famiglia dell'anima è sparsa in tutto il mondo, costruendo comunità veramente indipendenti, sostenibili e felici tra cui saltare, su e giù, muovendosi con le stagioni, come si muovono gli animali e le tribù indigene—in armonia con l'universo e il flusso naturale della vita, perché questo è il nuovo, anche se vecchio principio, il modello originale della vita?! Forse non mi stabilisco mai perché il mondo deve essere esplorato prima di stabilirsi. Forse non mi fermo mai in un posto perché il mondo è troppo bello per vivere in un solo posto, perché siamo una grande famiglia felice, con tanti tratti e colori diversi che si completano a vicenda per assaggiare sapori, paesaggi e culture diverse?! Forse non sono seduta qui da sola, con una casa, un marito e dei figli, perché amo tutti i bambini del mondo e non devo chiamarne uno mio, forse perché non voglio mai più avere questo tipo di relazione antiquata e noiosa, occupandomi della casa e del giardino 365 giorni all'anno, legata a un solo luogo, che mi limiterebbe e perché mai dovrei preoccuparmi di come, quando, cosa, dove, invece di cavalcare questa brillante onda della vita amici miei?!

Monti Metalliferi, Germania, Maggio 2023

Cultura cosmica

Non mi identifico con la cultura tedesca. Non credo di identificarmi con nessuna cultura. Vivo davvero la mia cultura e prendo il meglio da ogni cultura che ho sperimentato. Certo, ho tratto grande ispirazione da culture diverse e ho riconosciuto alcuni miei tratti in altre culture, ma così come ogni concetto creato dall'uomo, la cultura ha i suoi limiti, ma io sono senza limiti e atipica perché sono deprogrammata, cioè libera. Amo la franchezza tedesca, l'eccentricità britannica, la giocosità italiana, la scioltezza spagnola e la *coolness* africana, ecc. ma gli stili di vita non sono così diversi al giorno d'oggi in un mondo in cui le persone sono guidate principalmente dal denaro. Anche nei luoghi più remoti, dove una mente creativa può avere mille idee come realizzarsi, la gente continua a lavorare come un robot. Come si può essere così estremamente programmati, mi chiedo? È questa mentalità fatta di soldi e orari che ti permette di avere dalle 4 alle 6 settimane di ferie pagate dalla tua vita, bla bla. Capisco che è impossibile vivere così con una mente risvegliata. Nessuno è migliore di un altro ma quando si è coscienti, il denaro non è altro che un sottoprodotto. Come possiamo dimenticare che è solo un mezzo per raggiungere un fine? Come puoi permettergli di assumere il ruolo principale nella tua vita? Come hai potuto diventare così dipendente dal materialismo, come hai potuto dimenticare ciò che sapevi da bambino? Qual è la tua passione? Cosa creerai? Ci troveremo e costruiremo il nuovo insieme. Con la nostra tribù dell'anima e inventeremo una nuova moneta, un nuovo lusso, una sorta di magia.

Monti Metalliferi, Germania, Maggio 2023

Casa II

Ritorno a casa
E nessuno potrà mai bandirmi di nuovo
Dalla mia terra
Dove sono venuta
Perché tutto ciò che sono
È in piena vista
Mai più nascosto
E se non si adatta alle vostre menti recintate
Non odierò più
Perché ci giro sopra
Nel mio mondo libero
Dove sfondo i vostri muri di paura
Con amore

Monti Metalliferi, Germania, Maggio 2023

Giardino libero

Ho viaggiato in così tanti paesi e ho incontrato e vissuto con così tante nazionalità diverse che, invece di diventare come uno qualsiasi di loro, invece di amarne uno e odiarne un altro, diventi sempre più te stesso. Ci si rende conto che molto di ciò che si vede negli altri è una programmazione culturale, non il modo in cui le persone sono nate—libere—e più si allarga il quadro, più si diventa saggio e calmo. Si diventa osservatori. Alcune culture ti ispirano e altre tendono a respingerti, a seconda di ciò che si adatta al tuo carattere e fuggi da ciò che non ti si addice finché non ti rendi conto che l'unica cosa da cui puoi fuggire è te stesso. Hai imparato che puoi odiare solo ciò che fa parte di te fino a quando non c'è più nulla da odiare. Il modo in cui i sistemi di credenze, i sistemi sociali e politici funzionano e forgiano le persone possono frustrarti solo se prendi parte ad esse, ma il mondo non è un paese, un governo o una nazione che ti possieda. Si tratta di concetti artificiali basati sulla separazione, sulla classificazione e nati dalle vecchie energie di potere e di controllo che non possono più controllarti o esautorarti quando comprendi che il mondo è un giardino libero di abbondanza in cui puoi fiorire e danzare e che sei sempre tu a creare la tua realtà attraverso le tue convinzioni e che hai il libero arbitrio di scegliere ciò a cui partecipi e ciò a cui non partecipi. Non esiste un paese, un sistema o una nazione perfetta, ma la terra è bella e divina ovunque, il resto è una nostra creazione. Mi sono chiesta tante volte perché ho scelto di incarnarmi in un paese che mi sembrava il meno libero rispetto a tutti gli altri luoghi che ho visto e con i tedeschi che sembrano così limitati e intrappolati nelle loro menti perfettamente organizzate, che di conseguenza portano a una mancanza di cuore, di passione e di gioia, e ho capito che era una delle mie più grandi sfide e la missione del mio cuore scegliere questo paese. Per me casa non è mai stata un paese, una nazione o il concetto culturale di un luogo, ma nient'altro che la terra libera—l'energia della terra, i campi e le foreste, l'essenza della natura e del mito, l'amore, la tradizione e il rifugio—il luogo che chiamo casa e che non conosce confini di libertà e amore. E mi rendo conto che amo anche tutto ciò che qui ha cercato di togliermi la libertà, perché è così che me la sono ripresa completamente e perché il mio sogno era mostrare al mondo come essere libero, come una apripista, una visionaria, come una pioniera. Per amore.

Monti Metalliferi, Germania, Giugno 2023

Madre Terra

Da bambina, i nostri genitori e nonni portavano spesso me e mia sorella a raccogliere funghi nei grandi boschi dei Monti Metalliferi dove ci immergevamo profondamente per ore senza parlare molto, dove diventavamo parte del nostro ambiente e ricordo di aver provato una profonda venerazione per la grande foresta mitica e ancora oggi faccio lo stesso e mi rende davvero felice. Se sei cresciuto nell'ex DDR come me, l'autosufficienza era abbastanza normale, quasi tutti coltivavano un orto e avevano animali con cui vivere. Ora l'intero movimento della permacultura e dell'off-grid è diventato quasi una moda in risposta a una vita di città orientata al consumo e scollegata dalla natura, e non mi piacciono né l'uno né l'altro estremo. Per me vivere nella natura è la cosa più normale del mondo, probabilmente perché sono cresciuta in campagna dove è normale conoscere piante commestibili, bacche e funghi, motivo per cui ho sempre trovato ridicoli i parchi e le aree gioco.

Invece di visitare la natura come una turista, sono sempre tornata a vivere in mezzo alla natura e ho sempre osservato e imparato da essa. È la mia più grande ispirazione, la mia più grande guaritrice e maestra. L'umanità ha dimenticato che lei è la terra su cui poggi, l'aria che respiri, la casa in cui vivi, la pace e l'equilibrio che trovi dentro di te. Rispetta tua madre. Madre Terra.

Monti Metalliferi, Germania, Luglio 2023

Estate mia

Estate mia
Quanto pesi
E non mi piace più parlare
Gli alberi sussurrano
Le foglie ondeggiano
Le erbe danzano
Nella luce della sera
Perché non riesci a vederli?
Estate mia, ti amo così tanto.

Monti Metalliferi, Germania, Luglio 2023

Coraggiosa e libera

Sono davvero orgogliosa di me stessa per aver fatto quasi tutti i miei viaggi da sola, di aver iniziato a viaggiare all'estero in giovane età, di aver dormito in macchina sotto le stelle e in mille letti diversi, di non aver mai aspettato che il principe azzurro mi portasse in giro, di aver rifiutato quasi tutti gli inviti a vacanze di lusso da parte di ragazzi con un preciso scopo e di aver fatto cento lavori diversi per finanziare i miei viaggi. Ho conosciuto un sacco di persone speciali in giro per il mondo e ho sperimentato cose m*rdose, la vita vera, nei suoi estremi, superando le mie stesse paure e i miei limiti, crescendo di intere vite con l'adrenalina che ti scorre nel corpo su quell'unico e solo taxi da prendere sul retro di una moto attraverso le favelas di Rio con quel ragazzo del posto con quegli ipnotici occhi verdi per vedere Gesù. Potrei raccontare un milione di storie e non ho ancora finito.

Monti Metalliferi, Germania, Luglio 2023

IV. Verso est

Fame di inspirazione

Sono felice di aver fatto un nuovo salto, uscendo dal mio piccolo rifugio sicuro, il mio paradiso naturale nascosto nella campagna della Germania dell'Est con la mia famiglia e i miei amici che amo profondamente, ma dove tutti vivono lo stile di vita occidentale nella corsia di sorpasso—vivendo per lavorare completamente accecati dal mondo materiale e completamente disconnessi dallo spirito e mi manca terribilmente la vera ispirazione dalle persone che hanno integrato nella loro vita una pratica spirituale e un equilibrio tra lavoro e vita privata—la felicità—che studiano i misteri del cosmo invece delle occasioni di shopping e dei post di Instagram di oggi e non vedo l'ora di trovarli in Asia centrale. Sento che un grande spazio divino e aperto e gente sorridente mi chiamano e li troverò con la bussola del mio cuore.

Mascat, Oman, Agosto 2023

Tibet libero

In un incontro speciale con due tibetani nella vivace piazza principale del Nepal, sui scalini di uno dei tanti splendidi templi, che è una folle fusione tra la caotica vita quotidiana di Kathmandu e la sua affascinante vita spirituale, sento di aver imparato più di quanto alcune persone riescano a fare nei loro ashram e ritiri spirituali in diverse settimane—attraverso il più bel sorriso, l'amore e la leggerezza che la piccola bambina tibetana irradiava insieme a suo padre che mi ha dato un libro fatto a mano in tibetano che io non sono in grado di leggere, con tante illustrazioni Kamasutra, e attraverso l'incantevole suono del flauto dei bambini, il cui suono è il più alto e gioioso che io abbia mai sentita, e che ho seguito in uno dei templi, sentendo l'anima della cultura tibetana più di quanto avrei potuto fare in un costoso tour organizzato e supervisionato di gruppi di turisti—l'unico modo per andare in Tibet—e che ho deciso di rifiutare perché i soldi per questo sarebbero andati al governo cinese, che sta distruggendo la cultura tibetana e costringendo migliaia di persone all'esilio. Non importa quanto sia dura la vita—il Nepal è uno dei paesi più poveri del mondo—e quanto siano ingiusti e corrotti coloro che governano il mondo, corri libero e felice come la bambina tibetana.

Kathmandu, Nepal, Agosto 2023

Non possono conquistare la santità

Sono fortunata che la luce e l'acqua corrente non si vengano a mancare qui nella mia stanza da 3 dollari a Pokhara, dove mi trovo ai piedi degli 8000 metri della catena montuosa dell'Annapurna, come a Kathmandu, da dove sono arrivata con il peggior viaggio di 8 ore in autobus della mia vita lungo l'autostrada principale del paese e poi ho deciso di prendere un volo per tornare nella capitale perché non volevo cadere per centinaia di metri dalla strada sterrata nel letto del fiume, come spesso accade qui. Perché il Nepal è uno dei paesi più poveri del mondo nonostante il business milionario della scalata dell'Everest, che costa tra i 40000 e i 100000 dollari, con centinaia di scalatori a settimana?! Sedersi nei templi e imitare Buddha non è sufficiente se vogliamo fermare i leader corrotti di questo mondo. Bisogna alzarsi e riprendersi il proprio potere. Non conquistando il sacro Himalaya, ma stando e agendo nel tuo sacro potere dall'interno. Sono ai piedi del sacro

Machhapuchre, una dei pochi picchi che non possono essere scalati. Non possono conquistare la santità.

Pokhara, Nepal, Settembre 2023

Risvegliati al tuo vero potere

Per me una vacanza è una pausa dalla ruota del criceto, una pausa dalla vita per la quale ti fanno pagare duramente, ma la vita è qualcosa di più che essere in servizio e fuori servizio. La vita è la realizzazione di se stessi e un vero viaggio è un percorso spirituale di scoperta di se stessi e del mondo, per la tua crescita e l'ispirazione sul sentiero dell'unità, mentre impari più di quanto possano insegnarti. L'autorealizzazione è il tuo destino di vivere qualunque siano i tuoi doni, i tuoi talenti e le tue passioni e il denaro è un sottoprodotto di ciò, niente di più che un mezzo per raggiungere un fine, piuttosto che l'obiettivo principale in un equilibrio tra lavoro e vita—ricorda di sorridere, meditare, cantare, pregare, camminare, mangiare, respirare, amare in unità con la madre terra e tutte le forme di vita, piuttosto che autodistruggerti. La signora che mi ospita sulle montagne nepalesi prende il mais, il tè e i pomodori dal suo orto per farli seccare al sole. Rifletto sul trauma occidentale mentre guardo le meraviglie del mondo—le cime dell'Himalaya dalla mia stanza che mi costa 5 dollari al giorno, mentre altri pensano che non potrebbero mai permettersi una vacanza in Nepal per la quale vogliono migliaia di dollari in un viaggio organizzato. Segui il programma o risvegliateti al tuo vero potere.

Annapurna, Himalaya, Nepal, Settembre 2023

Himalaya

Himalaya
Tu stai nella tua santa potenza, profondamente
radicata nella madre, con la tua corona in cielo
Non lotti per i tuoi diritti
Stando nella tua santa presenza
Ricordandomi chi sono
Om Namah Shivaya
Himalaya

Annapurna, Himalaya, Nepal, Settembre 2023

Il mio cuore nomade batte più forte

Il mio cuore nomade batte più forte da quando ho messo piede in Mongolia. Il mio cuore ha sempre desiderato vivere sotto il grande cielo della terra infinita, al ritmo degli elementi, delle stagioni, degli animali e del flusso naturale della vita—un amore davvero antico. Per tutta la vita sono stata più felice fuori, al di là delle piccole scatole di cemento, dei muri e delle cornici. In nessun luogo ci si sente più liberi che al risveglio in una yurta tradizionale, con decine di aquile che volteggiano sopra la testa e con l'aria più fresca che si sia mai respirata, sorvolando le infinite, serene e bellissime praterie sul dorso di un cavallo mongolo selvaggio. Per me è uno dei luoghi più ispiranti che abbia mai visitato, anche perché è il paese meno occidentalizzato e globalizzato che abbia mai conosciuto. Il popolo mongolo ha mantenuto la sua propria identità orgogliosa, forte, individuale e indipendente ed è la gente più dolce e simpatica che abbia mai incontrato: è incredibilmente ospitale, gentile, aperta e intelligente, grazie al suo stile di vita e al fatto che usa il proprio spirito critico invece di essere programmato dai media e dalle norme e dai vincoli sociali. Non sembrano affatto poveri, ma piuttosto ricchi e si vestono bene e in modo piuttosto cool—li vedi con questi lunghi e colorati cappotti di seta con una cintura e un cappello e occhiali da sole sulle loro moto d'epoca. Mi trovo nell'ex capitale dell'enorme, vasto e antico impero mongolo, cosa che ho scoperto solo quando ho visitato l'unico monastero buddista di Erdene Zuu del XVI secolo e vivo in una yurta che ho affittato da una simpatica famiglia locale, i cui figli sembrano molto maturi, indipendenti e intelligenti e che si occupano da soli dell'intera casa mentre il padre va in giro per la natura selvaggia per qualche giorno—cosa del tutto normale in Mongolia. Il paese ha solo tre milioni di abitanti, un terzo dei quali vive una vita nomade e le città hanno solo una manciata di negozi che vendono prodotti locali e ciò che è necessario, piuttosto che il consumo di massa e lo spreco. La vita nomade è di fatto il modo di vivere più sostenibile, responsabile e cosciente che esista, opposto a un arcaico modo di pensare coloniale occidentale di essere superiori ed è il futuro. Possedere poco, avere tutto. La libertà.

Kharkhorin, Mongolia, Settembre 2023

La via di mezzo

Sono molto orgogliosa di me stessa per aver trovato un modo di viaggiare per il mondo con pochi soldi, che mi ha permesso di evitare le principali trappole per turisti dove viene venduta un'immagine di un paese che ha poco a che fare con la realtà. So che le persone vanno in vacanza per prendersi una pausa dalla loro vita normale, dove cocktail e piscine probabilmente funzionano, ma io vivo una vita da cui non ho bisogno di una pausa e viaggio per l'avventura, per l'ispirazione e per ampliare le mie vedute. Sono sempre alla ricerca dell'esperienza locale e quindi mi trattano come uno di loro, il che mi tocca davvero il cuore quando mi rendo conto di essere importante per gli stranieri e di essere accolto a braccia aperte, cosa che ho sperimentato tante volte in giro per il mondo, soprattutto in luoghi dove la vera comunità conta ancora di più del denaro. Per conoscere davvero i luoghi stranieri, è necessario mescolarsi con la gente del posto e qui in Mongolia questo avviene da solo, perché le persone sono così calorose e aperte, cosa deriva dal loro stile di vita e dalle loro tribù nomadi—niente apre di più il cuore e la mente. Sono stata abbracciata dai bambini più dolci, invitata nelle case, ho condiviso il cibo, ho scambiato tanti sorrisi e comunicato con il linguaggio dei segni e soprattutto con il linguaggio del cuore che tutti capiscono. Non ho mai visto bambini così aperti, amichevoli, liberi e felici. Credo che tutti i bambini siano così per natura, ma l'educazione trasforma molti di loro in bambini timorosi, intimiditi o addirittura cattivi. Qui li vedi giocare tutti insieme all'aperto e ti sorridono automaticamente quando ti vedono, mentre dalle mie parti distoglierebbero lo sguardo. Qui mi sono venuti incontro con i loro cuori grandi e curiosi. Mi hanno dato da mangiare dei pinoli, hanno fatto delle foto con la mia Nikon, mi hanno abbracciato e non hanno smesso di parlarmi, anche se non capivo nulla se non: 'Dove sono i tuoi genitori?' Crescere nella natura, in comunità e con gli animali ha enormi effetti positivi sui bambini. I bambini incredibilmente spensierati, leggeri, gioiosi e liberi mi hanno toccato profondamente e mi hanno ricordato di essere come loro, di uscire a giocare e divertirmi e di non prendere la vita così seriamente. Ho notato anche una pratica spirituale sana e leggera in Mongolia—non una programmazione religiosa estrema come quella che ho osservato in altri paesi, ma in modo naturale—lo chiamo buddismo leggero o sano e mi rendo conto che abbiamo le stesse credenze senza che io l'abbia mai studiato sui libri, ma scoprendo io stessa le sue grandi verità universali camminando sul sentiero del cuore e scoprendo me stessa e il mondo. Vedere in Asia persone che cantano e danzano i loro mantra sui marciapiedi, che parlano con le loro divinità mentre cucinano o che siedono a meditare nelle strade e nelle piazze è la cosa più normale del mondo, mentre saresti considerato un pazzo se facessi lo stesso in Occidente. La Mongolia mi ispira, soprattutto perché ho notato come qui la gente usa ancora il proprio spirito critico, a differenza della programmazione del mondo occidentale che segue ciecamente la matrice, mentre qui la vita è naturale, piena di senso e di anima. Genuino.

Kharkhorin, Mongolia, Settembre 2023

Cavalcata nella libertà

Ieri ho ingaggiato uno del posto in moto per portarmi in montagna, indicandogli la direzione che sembrava affascinante e che non era una buona idea percorrere a piedi, perché tutto ciò che sembra vicino in Mongolia è molto lontano. Abbiamo comunicato nel linguaggio dei segni e gli ho dato 10 dollari perché questo è il modo in cui ho imparato a viaggiare per il motivo originario, cosa che non ho mai avuto molti soldi, che mi ha salvato dal cadere nelle principali trappole per turisti e dove ho imparato a essere coraggiosa, a usare il buon senso, a osservare ciò che mi circonda e ad ascoltare il mio intuito, che è meglio di qualsiasi guida turistica pagata al mondo e la migliore garanzia per l'avventura e per conoscere davvero un paese per quello che è, piuttosto che attraverso una falsa immagine venduta ai turisti, e mi ha dato l'opportunità di imparare e crescere al di là di me stessa nel modo più grande, piuttosto che spuntare su una lista le attrazioni che gli altri ritengono importanti!

Il mio conducente mi ha portato nel posto più bello e nascosto, con un'energia incredibilmente chiara, dove i monaci hanno costruito alcuni piccoli templi buddisti, riconoscendo la montagna come sacra. Durante il viaggio attraverso le ampie praterie, ho incrociato yurte nomadi, cammelli e un sacco di pecore e capre, mentre il mio simpatico conducente canticchiava alcune canzoni e io pensavo 'Potrei vivere qui', *lol*. Chi supera la paura dell'ignoto avrà in dono la più grande libertà, divertimento e magia.

Kharkhorin, Mongolia, Settembre 2023

Terra di libertà

Mongolia
Il mio cuore desiderava la terra della libertà
Che ho riconosciuto
Attraverso la fiamma che ardeva dentro di me
Che si è accesa come mai prima
Quando ho rivisto la steppa e le praterie infinite
Scintillanti nella luce dorata
Dove solo l'orizzonte chiama il mio nome
Dove ci sediamo accanto al fuoco sotto un
milione di stelle
Condividendo i nostri cuori
Amore eterno
Per la terra della libertà
Che brucia per sempre

Kharkhorin, Mongolia, Settembre 2023

Una volta ero uno sciamano

So che
In un'altra vita
Ero uno sciamano
Da qualche parte tra la magica steppa mongola
e le profonde foreste della Siberia
Potevo volare con le aquile, correre con i cavalli,
danzare con gli spiriti
Potevo fare qualsiasi cosa
Ora taglio tutte le catene che tengono
prigioniera l'umanità
Le vecchie torri del potere e del controllo
stanno cadendo
La Nuova Terra fiorisce e tutti i suoi figli tornano
a correre liberi

Kharkhorin, Mongolia, Settembre 2023

Nomade per natura

Pensavo che l'anno prossimo avrei viaggiato di meno, ma come si fa a fermarsi una volta che si è assaggiata la libertà? Ciò che mi ispira di più al mondo sono le persone genuine, amichevoli, positive, aperte e ho incontrato così tante persone di buon cuore durante i miei viaggi in giro per il mondo, e molto spesso qui in Mongolia, dove mi hanno semplicemente reso parte di loro, invitandomi a sedermi e mangiare con loro, quando mi hanno visto aspettare un autobus sul ciglio della strada in mezzo al nulla, mi hanno portato personalmente all'altro capo della capitale Ulan Bator quando ho chiesto indicazioni e tutti gli altri dolci incontri che non dimenticherò mai—condivideranno tutto con te dove il capitalismo e l'egoismo non hanno ancora corrotto i cuori. Anche se il mio aspetto è diverso dal loro, qui non ti giudicano per il tuo aspetto, ma ti riconoscono come un viaggiatore che accolgono a braccia aperte e non c'è alcuna intenzione dietro le loro azioni se non quella della compassione e dell'amore—il completo opposto della cultura in cui sono nata e per la quale non vorrei mai vivere lì a tempo pieno—ma solo andare e stare come un nomade nella sua yurta sulla terra aperta, quando e dove è guidato dalla natura, dalla sua intuizione e dalla sua saggezza.

Kharkhorin, Mongolia, Settembre 2023

Anima della Siberia

Brezza sacra
Porta foglie dorate di allegre betulle
Cospargendo il tappeto di morbida sabbia
Alla tua riva lavata
Dalle tue acque cristalline
Dalle profondità della tua anima
Dove io sola danzo
Con gli spiriti
Nelle foreste inondate di luce di larici e pini
Santo Baikal
Qui e ovunque
Creazione gloriosa
Celebrare

Maksimikha, Lago Baikal, Siberia, Russia, 2023

Autostop a Goryachinsk

Ho fatto l'autostop fino a Goryachinsk. Lago Baikal, lato est, dove la Transiberiana non sputa fuori i turisti stranieri che non vengono più, ma dove sono tutto sola con i pochi locali. Non c'è niente di più autentico. È meglio che lascio i gioielli in camera. Anche la macchina fotografica. Non si sa mai. Quando si viaggia da solo per il mondo, si impara a non correre questo rischio. Altri ne devi correre. Come viaggiare in Russia, quando la chiamata è più forte della paura che cercano di diffondere. Viaggiare da soli in Siberia è più sicuro di qualsiasi grande città del mio paese d'origine, la Germania, e quando si viaggia da soli per il mondo si perde la paura, ci si fida sempre di più del proprio intuito e si diventa forti sul proprio cammino e soave nel proprio cuore. Ovunque tu vada, le persone sono gentili con te perché lo sei tu e ti senti infinitamente libero. Ogni giorno porta una nuova scoperta su di sé e sul mondo. Il lago Baikal, il più profondo, antico e limpido lago del mondo, è una meraviglia: bisogna viverlo nella sua saggezza e potenza, circondato da una fitta e sconfinata foresta di taiga e la Siberia è siberiana. Magica e solitaria. C'è più vodka che cibo fresco, si mangia grano saraceno al posto del riso, le case sono di legno, le tovaglie sono fatte all'uncinetto e la gente pensa che io sia russa finché non inizio a parlare. Se non è accogliente, allora è squallido. Un intermezzo, come la vita stessa. Molte persone si trasferiscono in città finché non capiscono che la vita lì è ancora più solitaria che in Siberia se non vi porgete le mani—non cadere nella trappola del capitalismo—l'idea di giustizia sociale di Lenin era buona, ma non aveva capito che non può essere dettata dall'alto, ma sorge dal basso—dalla profonda comprensione dentro di te che siamo tutti uguali e che il vero potere sta nel tuo cuore e nelle tue mani e quando vedi la bellezza invece della solitudine del tuo villaggio siberiano—la tua libertà è la tua indipendenza. Tutti qui sanno che la guerra è un affare dei governanti del mondo, ma loro non hanno potere se non glielo dai tu.

Turka, Lago Baikal, Siberia, Russia, Ottobre 2023

La libertà

Chiunque può sedersi al bar di un hotel e ordinare un cocktail, ma non tutti sopportano la solitudine. Tu da solo in un posto dove nessuno vuole andare perché nessuno ne ha mai parlato in una guida turistica. Le persone sono come le pecore. Seguono ciecamente il gregge, ma io sono come un lupo solitario che segue il proprio istinto di scoprire il mondo e sceglie saggiamente il proprio gregge. L'uomo di città atterra su un autobus nella bellezza della natura selvaggia e la sua prima osservazione sarà: qui non c'è niente. Il lupo capisce che il nulla è tutto. Sente gli elementi parlare, il vento, le onde, gli alberi, gli altri animali e si siede in silenzio ad ascoltare il nulla che rivela la sua magia a chi ascolta al di là del tempo. Il silenzio parla. Non ha bisogno di un recinto intorno a sé per sentirsi al sicuro, ama vagare nell'immensità. Confida di incontrare un amico come lui.

Turka, Lago Baikal, Siberia, Russia, Ottobre 2023

Rituale sciamanico

In Asia è abbastanza comune osservare la pratica spirituale nella vita quotidiana. Si vedono persone che cantano i loro mantra all'aperto, che entrano in meditazione ovunque in pubblico, che stanno in piedi vicino all'autostrada con una ciotola di latte assorte in una profonda preghiera o che ti fanno partecipare a un rituale sciamanico, come mi è successo oggi. Un gruppo di amici della tribù locale dei Buryat, che ha una tradizione sciamanica molto forte, mi ha fatto cenno di avvicinarmi mentre camminavo nella foresta lungo le rive del lago Baikal e quando mi hanno visto seduto su una roccia ad ascoltare i loro tamburi. Mi hanno dato del *chai* e degli snack da mangiare, che avevano con sé. Il lago Baikal e gli spiriti sono stati venerati cantando e ricevendo in dono vodka, grandi torte, sigarette, vestiti, tè e altro ancora. La sciamana—una sciamana di nascita e una ragazza normale e non un guru narcisista, occidentale e costoso che parlava con gli spiriti della natura—è entrata in trance e ha convogliato lo spirito benedicendo tutti i membri del gruppo. In modo molto naturale, sono stata resa parte della cerimonia—qualsiasi sia il mio background, la mia provenienza o le mie convinzioni—semplicemente perché ero lì, guidata dallo spirito, come sempre, naturalmente. È stato un sogno diventato realtà. Sono molto attratta da questa cultura perché collega lo spirito con la natura, la creatività, la musica e la danza. È molto più bello che sedersi in una chiesa ed essere trasformati in peccatore. È bello e commovente vedere le persone che condividono la loro religione con te e parlano con lo spirito e i loro dei nella vita quotidiana. Se facessi qualcosa di simile in pubblico in Germania, mi darebbero della pazza in una cultura che si è completamente separata dallo spirito e ha dimenticato la sua vera natura di parte del tutto. Danza, preghiera, natura, espressione, comunità. Natura cosmica umana.

Turka, Lago Baikal, Siberia, Russia, Ottobre 2023

Masterclass spirituale

Questo viaggio in Asia non è solo una delle mie più grandi avventure, in cui mi immergo nelle culture più diverse che mi ispirano e illuminano i miei orizzonti nel modo più assoluto, ma è anche una masterclass spirituale. Da un lato c'è Tokyo, dove mi sono sentita come in un film apocalittico—la *matrix* con le sue persone robotizzate che si muovono in perfetto ordine tra un mare infinito di grattacieli e poi c'è quest'altro Giappone—un'altra realtà che sa di reale, con le sue montagne lussureggianti e il Feng Shui, c'è il Taoismo e l'energia Qi in cui mi sento immersa. Ci sono così tanti insegnamenti diversi in questo mondo e osservo come molti studenti diventino discepoli devoti—schiavi—di una dottrina, che si tratti dei monaci buddisti o degli *hippie New Age*. Ai miei occhi, la pratica spirituale assume spesso una forma troppo estrema. A mio parere, non è qualcosa da vivere da sola, ma da applicare nella vita quotidiana. Per me non si tratta di dimostrare che una sistema di credenze o un'altra hanno completamente ragione. Questi sono i limiti dei sistemi di credenze, spesso legati al bisogno narcisistico di avere ragione e quando una dottrina vuole che tu sia un seguace convinto, non è più saggia, ma depotenziante, controllo. Invece di diventare un seguace di una corrente o di un'altra, ho studiato i misteri della vita attraverso l'introspezione e l'osservazione dell'esterno, di me stessa e nei miei viaggi intorno al mondo e ho ricevuto una grande quantità di conoscenza e saggezza, la maggior parte delle quali ho assorbito energeticamente e attraverso l'osservazione, piuttosto che essere un seguace di qualcuno che deve avere ragione e sono entusiasta di ciò che sto ricevendo. Non mi convertirò all'induismo, al buddismo o al taoismo, così come non mi sono convertito al protestantesimo o sono diventata un *hippie New Age*, ma ho integrato molti aspetti diversi perché non sono né l'uno né l'altro, ma tutto quello che mi ha ispirato ed emozionato immensamente perché sono parti della mia anima cosmica. I luoghi possono avere energia che trasporta informazioni dalla luce o dai paesaggi e poi ci sono luoghi della matrice senza energia come le grandi città dove le persone si muovono come robot in uno schema e ciò che sembra un film apocalittico e poi c'è questo sogno. Quest'altra realtà. Il paradiso in terra. Posso incanalare la saggezza e la conoscenza degli alberi, dell'energia di un luogo, della musica o dei templi o delle pietre che hanno tutti una certa energia che puoi raccogliere invece di diventare uno studente di migliaia di libri scritti da altri — ho letto migliaia di pagine durante i miei studi universitari e ora scrivo i miei libri, che non parlano di me, ma sono scritti per te, per ricordarti di te stesso.

Oshino Hakkai, Giappone, Ottobre 2023

Fujiyama

Campi di fiori di bambù argentati risplendono
ai tuoi piedi in lontananza
Oggi nascondi il tuo bianco cappello di
neve tra nubi
Non riuscivo a trovare la strada
Poi sono uscita in bicicletta e mi sono sdraiata in
un prato vicino a un ruscello
C'era un ponte
Con fiori di bambù dall'altra parte
Ho attraversato il ponte
E tu eri molto vicino a me
Fujiyama
Hai soffiato via le nuvole

Oshino Hakkai, Giappone, Ottobre 2023

Spettacolo apocalittico

Tokyo
Tu chiudi i tuoi parchi a pagamento di notte
e porti la gente in autobus la domenica per
visitare la natura recintata, gettare monete nei
santuari e andare a caccia di souvenir.
È di moda andare in giro come una copia di un
finto re o regina dei fumetti.
Gli alberi parlano più forte, i draghi ridono
e le catene montuose si ergono sopra i tuoi
grattacieli.
Il tuo futuro si sente apocalittico, baby!

Tokyo, Giappone, Ottobre 2023

Eroina del Tam Coc

Mangia come un abitante del posto, il che significa minestra di pasta vietnamita a colazione, perché rimarrai enormemente deluso da alcune imitazioni del cibo occidentale fatte apposta per i turisti internazionali di questa parte del mondo—no, io non sono una di loro! La maggior parte di loro si raggruppa negli stessi hotel, ristoranti e luoghi di attività, seguendo le recensioni e le raccomandazioni online, fissando i loro telefoni mentre attraversano la strada—mi chiedo quanti vengano travolti dalla marea di moto—non un passo senza Google Maps—mai senza il telefono, ma hai dimenticato come si fa una telefonata. L'eroe/ eroina non è l'Instagrammer del Banana Tree Swimming Pool hotel, ma la signora vietnamita che, insieme agli altri sulla sua barca, porta ogni giorno centinaia di turisti in un luogo un tempo incantevole nella natura che è stato prosciugato—un tipo di turismo non inclusivo, non sostenibile e incentrato sul profitto—io lo chiamo neocolonialismo—che non sostengo. No, questo non è il Vietnam! Il suo fascino antico esiste ancora—l'ho trovato nei sorrisi sui visi e negli angoli dove nessuno guarda e mentre voi rincorrete l'autobus per la vostra prossima fermata o per il prossimo tempio buddista, io sono sdraiata qui sotto il sole, circondata dalle bellissime rocce del Tam Coc, osservando le foglie che cadono, i fiori e le farfalle, vivendo la via buddista che è in ogni momento. Non essere un seguace, sii un condottiero. Un condottiero del cuore.

Tam Coc, Vietnam, Ottobre 2023

Lei tiene la chiave

Il mio bellissimo, gentile, innocente Vietnam. Ho visto la tua anima e mi sono innamorata di te l'ultimo giorno dopo che mi hai insegnato tutte le dure lezioni che dovevo imparare. Ora mi sento come una regina che si rotola nel tuo verde giardino tropicale di banane, palme da cocco e bambù nel suo letto di lusso, che in realtà è un autobus, ma non importa più, e sono libera, liberamente fluttuante, finalmente libera da tutta la pesantezza e il dolore del vecchio mondo, libera per sempre. Questo viaggio non è sicuramente un viaggio turistico. È un'evoluzione spirituale, un crescere insieme nell'amore. Ci sono così tanti flussi e riflussi, storie da raccontare, sfide da affrontare, ponti da attraversare, epifanie da avere e anime preziose da incontrare lungo la strada. Dopo tutto questo, ci si rende conto che l'unica cosa che conta è il momento, che è tutto ciò che si ha. Buono o cattivo che sia, abbraccialo, vivilo, senza giudicarlo o pensarci troppo. Vivilo e basta. Ed eccola lì. La piccola, bellissima ragazza che tiene la chiave.

Sapa, Vietnam, Novembre 2023

Atterrare in India

Atterrare in India dopo 10 settimane in Asia è una sensazione bellissima!!! Come una celebrazione. Il mio tassista mi ha lasciato da qualche parte nel folle centro di Varanasi, dove ho avuto un passaggio in moto fino ai gradini del fiume Gange—il luogo più sacro dell'India, dove si vedono i corpi morti bruciare e i pellegrini fare il bagno nel fiume che ha quell'atmosfera da pelle d'oca con tutti i templi, le cerimonie, le candele e le barche. Mi sento molto ben accolta dagli adorabili abitanti del luogo che dicono che aiutare fa bene al karma—amano mostrarti la strada attraverso il labirinto di mille bazar, rishka, biciclette, moto e persone e l'hashish fa bene al kamasutra, *lol*. Anche se qui prendono la loro fede molto seriamente, c'è gioia nell'aria e non sento affatto il bisogno di coprirmi, tanto meno a 30 gradi come mi avevano detto di fare in India. Nessuna argomentazione al mondo giustifica la necessità per una donna di coprirsi e per un uomo di non farlo, e otterrai più rispetto se sarai ciò che sei veramente piuttosto che professare le credenze e gli stigmi altrui. Abito lungo o abito corto, agli dei non importa davvero.

Varanasi, India, Novembre 2023

Sono la maestra della manifestazione dei miei sogni

Sono la maestra della manifestazione dei miei sogni. Questo significa che devi colorare esattamente e senza alcun dubbio i desideri del tuo cuore per riceverli, perché non dovresti ricevere ciò che sogni e poi darli all'universo e ti saranno dati. È quello che ho fatto io. Desideravo un posto a Goa senza rumori, senza branchi di *hippie New Age* o turisti, in una bella casa fresca sotto le palme, con un letto fantastico e una terrazza proprio sull'oceano, ed è quello che ho ottenuto. È spuntata oggi mentre camminavo lungo la spiaggia—così un pescatore mi ha portato lì dopo che abbiamo chiacchierato di fronte alla sua baracca sulla spiaggia, tra le barche da pesca e i fiori che amo così tanto e dove la gente del posto ama condividere il suo cibo con me e mi tratta come una famiglia. Non volevo stare in una piccola baia a forma di mezzaluna, orlata di palme, ingombra di un centinaio di lettini, capanne, alberghi e persone, con mille storie e questa animazione rumorosa per persone che non sopportano il silenzio, non sopportano la vita, non sopportano se stessi, che hanno bisogno di un programma costante, che non hanno alcuna comprensione della natura e tutto ciò che sento dalla mia stanza è il suono dell'oceano. Ho dovuto riascoltare la terra e il cosmo. La mia più grande ispirazione. Qui siamo solo io e i pescatori—spesso mi offrono la cena direttamente dalla barca—e l'ampio, aperto, caldo, magico, potente, bellissimo Oceano Indiano. Dovevo stare vicino all'oceano. L'oceano è la mia animazione. Cura la mia anima, purifica il mio corpo, mi riempie di forza, di vita.

Colva, Goa, India, Novembre 2023

Rinata

Ed è dopo 18 paesi che hai viaggiato in tre continenti solo quest'anno, una grande missione in cui sei stata spinta e che è stata facilitata dalle forze dell'Universo seguendo la bussola del tuo cuore, dopo 18 vite che hai vissuto in un solo anno, dopo un'immersione profonda in tutte le diverse culture, dimensioni e tempi, c'è il momento improvviso del completamento—e la gioia inizia a penetrare in ogni vostra cellula e si riflette nel gioco e nelle risate dei bambini, nelle danze notturne sulla tua terrazza al ritmo del vicino *beach club* sotto le palme da cocco nella brezza dell'oceano in bikini, riflessa nelle barche da pesca che disegnano insieme il rosso del tramonto indiano al largo, una gioia e una spensieratezza che ti mancavano e che non vorrai mai più perdere e che porterai con te ovunque andrai. Sei rinata. È nel momento in cui lasci andare tutte le vecchie convinzioni che la vita sia dura e difficile, quando sblocchi il flusso cosmico di amore e vita che senti scorrere nel tuo corpo. Nel momento in cui sai che crei il tuo sogno in ogni istante, crei qualsiasi cosa sogni, nel momento in cui fluisci. Continuate a cavalcare l'onda cosmica dell'amore e della vita, che è sempre lì per saltare sopra, amici miei.

Colva, Goa, India, Novembre 2023

Bombay Love

Sono felice di non aver avuto i soldi per soggiornare nel leggendario Taj Mahal Palace hotel, dove i soldi spesi in un giorno potrebbero far uscire dalla povertà tutta l'India, ma di averti abbracciato in un vecchio e degradato hotel coloniale a cinque piani di fronte al Taj Mahal, appoggiata alla finestra, guardando sotto la luna piena che sorgeva nel cielo caldo e dorato della sera indiana qui a Bombay. Solo l'amore può renderti reale. Ti fa passare attraverso il portale dall'illusione alla realtà, dall'ombra alla luce. Ti fa tornare a essere ciò che sei sempre stato. Amore.

Bombay, India, Novembre 2023

La vita è un sogno e tu sei l'autore

Sull'autrice

Janet Kaufmann è nata nell'ex DDR, nella Germania dell'Est, dove da bambina ha assistito alla caduta del Muro di Berlino. Si è laureata in Scienze dell'Educazione, Psicologia e Lingue straniere all'Università di Lipsia in Germania e all'Università Aix-Marsiglia in Francia. Oltre al tedesco, parla correntemente inglese, francese, spagnolo e italiano. Ha lavorato come insegnante di scuola e insegnante privata in Germania, Russia, Italia e Ungheria, nonché come giornalista per il dipartimento internazionale della televisione tedesca MDR e della televisione francese ARTE, oltre a molti altri lavori diversi in Germania, Francia, Spagna, Monaco, Inghilterra, Scozia e altro ancora per acquisire esperienza di vita e permettersi i suoi viaggi.

Ha scritto tre libri nelle cinque lingue che parla: *Age of Liberation* pubblicato nel 2021, *Taste of Freedom / L'Esprit de Liberté / Sabor a Libertad* pubblicato nel 2023 e *Like a Thrill / Wie ein Rausch / Alla corrente del vento* pubblicato nel 2024. Nei suoi libri, l'autrice racconta come si è liberata dalle convinzioni limitanti e dalle norme e dalle costrizioni della società e della cultura con un salto di fede che l'ha portata in giro per il mondo, sperimentando molti paesi e culture diverse. Ci mostra come raggiungere uno stato interiore di libertà, amore e coscienza dell'unità e ci ispira e incoraggia a vivere un nuovo modello di vita basato sulla libertà, l'indipendenza, la creatività e la comunità con un approccio olistico, invece di vivere una vita condizionata in una piccola scatola. I suoi libri sono accompagnati da avventure uniche, ispirazioni e messaggi incoraggianti per creare insieme nuovi modi di vivere, uscendo dal vecchio programma di paura, controllo e potere dall'alto. Ci mostra come possiamo elevarci, stare nel nostro potere e creare una vita felice autodeterminata e un mondo nuovo e migliore insieme.

Ha iniziato a viaggiare da giovane e ad oggi ha visitato quasi 60 paesi in Europa, Nord e Sud America, Africa e Asia. Oltre ai suoi viaggi in tutto il mondo, l'autrice vive oggi tra la Germania e l'India e si impegna in diversi progetti auto-sostenibili e creativi con la comunità locale, gli amici e la famiglia nel mondo. Come artista, espone le sue straordinarie fotografie da tutto il mondo in diversi luoghi e gallerie. Ha appena girato il suo primo cortometraggio in India. Desidera ispirare il mondo e impegnarsi in un cambiamento positivo attraverso la sua letteratura e le sue arti e la sua stile di vita libero e felice.

Nel Fuoco del Nostro Amore
Bruciarono le vecchie vie e il vecchio mondo fino
alle ceneri
Sparsi nelle acque sacre
Dove ci Eleviamo
Come una Nuova Legge Cosmica
Di Amore Divino

Other Books by Janet Kaufmann

Conscious Dreams
PUBLISHING

Transforming diverse writers
into successful published authors

www.consciousdreamspublishing.com

authors@consciousdreamspublishing.com

Let's connect